An Open World

An Open World

How America Can Win the Contest for Twenty-First-Century Order

Rebecca Lissner and Mira Rapp-Hooper

Yale UNIVERSITY PRESS

New Haven and London

Published with assistance from the foundation established in memory of Amasa Stone Mather of the Class of 1907, Yale College.

Yale University Press books may be purchased in quantity for educational, business, or promotional use. For information, please e-mail sales.press@yale.edu (U.S. office) or sales@yaleup.co.uk (U.K. office).

Set in Janson Roman type by IDS Infotech Ltd., Chandigarh, India. Printed in the United States of America.

Library of Congress Control Number: 2020932815
ISBN 978-0-300-25032-9 (hardcover : alk. paper)

A catalogue record for this book is available from the British Library.

This paper meets the requirements of ANSI/NISO Z39.48-1992 (Permanence of Paper).

10 9 8 7 6 5 4 3 2 1

Contents

Acknowledgments

This book project was born in a moment of historic upheaval. In the wake of a stunning election in November 2016, we sought to make sense of a political maelstrom that had few analogues, but seemed much more than a fleeting moment. As we developed a research agenda that would allow us to analyze the domestic and international forces afoot and propose a strategy to meet them, we had numerous supporters who shared in our inquiry and made our work possible. From the project's inception, Jake Sullivan and Jim Steinberg have provided invaluable guidance, serving as intellectual sounding boards, thoughtful reviewers, and tireless advocates. When our "Day After Trump" agenda was in its earliest days, Alex Lennon provided it a first home in the *Washington Quarterly*, and he has continued to lend his enthusiastic support. As we began developing the contours of the new American strategy we propose in this book, Dan Kurtz-Phelan at *Foreign Affairs* was just as supportive, continuing to offer thoughtful feedback throughout.

Our project has also received extraordinary institutional support and funding. As we developed our multi-year agenda, we had a true champion in Paul Gewirtz and the China Center at Yale Law School. Paul understood immediately what we hoped to accomplish and offered stalwart institutional backing and intellectual guidance. We were privileged to work with the Department of Defense's Office of Net Assessment as we conducted our domestic and international trend analysis, and our findings benefited immensely from Jim Baker, Andrew May, and Denise Der's thoughtful guidance. The later stages of our project were possible thanks to a generous grant from the Smith Richardson Foundation, and Marin Strmecki's wise counsel.

This book, ambitious in its scope and timeline, would have been impossible without tremendous research assistance. For that, we are grateful to Tyler Bowen, Dana Stuster, and Alexa Andaya. Special gratitude is owed to Laura Resnick Samotin and Don Casler, who made superb research contributions and supported this project for much of its duration. Finally, Kirk Lancaster helped us see this book to completion.

Our research proceeded in four major phases, and in each one we sought the input of other experts to review and strengthen our findings. We are grateful to the thoughtful participants in our November 2018 workshop "Domestic and International Trends and the Future of American Strategy"; to the superb country experts who provided feedback on Chinese, Russian, Indian, German, and Japanese approaches to order; to the extraordinary participants in our July 2019 "Grand Strategic Futures" workshop; and to the senior policy practitioners who provided sage counsel as we refined our strategy and policy recommendations.

At every stage, our work was buttressed by talented colleagues who lent their expertise and support to our initiative, including Emma Ashford, Beth Baltzan, Fritz Bartel, Stephen Beckwith, Hal Brands, Bill Burns, Jessica Chen Weiss, Matan Chorev, Tamara Cofman Wittes, Jared Cohen, Richard Connolley, Zack Cooper, Loren DeJonge Schulman, Dan Drezner, Elizabeth Economy, Charles Edel,

Acknowledgments

Ryan Evans, Michèle Flournoy, Bill Galston, Frank Gavin, Stacie Goddard, Jim Goldgeier, Zach Goldman, Stephen Hadley, Avril Haines, Gunther Hellmann, Susan Hennessey, Emily Holland, Mike Horowitz, Heather Hurlburt, Michael Hüther, Colin Jackson, Bruce Jentleson, Robert Jervis, Colin Kahl, Adam Liff, Rory MacFarquhar, Tanvi Madan, James Mattis, Chris Miller, Nuno Monteiro, Diana Mutz, Olga Oliker, Stewart Patrick, Radha Iyengar Plumb, Alina Polyakova, Chris Preble, Kirk Radke, Eric Reid, Eric Sayers, Kori Schake, Jackie Schneider, Robert Seamans, Adam Segal, Brad Setser, Sheila Smith, Paul Staniland, Constanze Stelzenmüller, Bruce Stokes, Matt Waxman, Tom Wright, Micah Zenko, and Philip Zelikow.

We are also indebted to the institutions that have been our professional homes during this research process. The Naval War College generously hosted our "Grand Strategic Futures" exercise, and Peter Dombrowski, Jonathan Caverley, Andrew Winner, and Rachael Shaffer provided superb guidance, facilitation, and logistical support as we designed and executed the scenario. At Yale's China Center, Concetta Fusco and Robert Williams have generously housed and helped to administer our project with care and enthusiasm. At the Council on Foreign Relations, we are grateful to Elizabeth Economy, Richard Haass, James Lindsay, and the talented communications team. At Yale University Press we were fortunate to work with Jaya Chatterjee and Eva Skewes; Robin DuBlanc and Margaret Otzel provided additional editorial and production guidance.

We are incredibly fortunate to have spouses who strengthen our work. From their enthusiasm for the project from its inception to their support as we held workshops and put in late nights writing to their willingness to occasionally perform the duties of research assistants, our book would have been impossible without Sam Lissner and Matthew Brest.

Our deepest gratitude extends to one another. This project commenced at a time of extraordinary global uncertainty, and has served as an intellectual anchor for us during a three-year period that was otherwise disorienting for foreign policy thinkers. During this time, we have also weathered momentous personal change: we moved homes, started new jobs, welcomed three children, and lost beloved family members. Our work continued because of our commitment to it and to one another. It is rare for two individuals to finish a coauthored project as closer friends than they were at the beginning; we are privileged to count each other as life-long collaborators and champions.

This book is dedicated to our children: Noah, Emilie, and Annelie. *An Open World* belongs to them.

Introduction

The Day After Trump

The election and inauguration of Donald Trump ricocheted through Washington's national security establishment, piercing the shibboleths to which it clung. On January 21, 2017, the new president sketched a dark portrait of a country that had prioritized its international agenda at grievous self-expense. His was a zero-sum vision in which global security and prosperity had cost the United States dearly. The "American carnage" could only be stopped with an inward turn. The message was hardly subtle: the postwar foreign policy of the prior seventy years, rooted in free-flowing commerce, cooperative multilateral institutions, and robust alliances, was now slain.

However dismal the picture, it was not entirely surprising. For months, scholars and analysts had mined Trump's campaign promises and long-held positions in search of coherent patterns that presaged a strategy to come. Trump blamed the nation's ills on "international unions that tie us up and bring America down." His denigration of allies, veneration of autocrats, and vilification of multilateral institutions and regimes were as heterodox as they were consistent—and they manifestly electrified a significant portion of the nation's populace. The judgment was therefore both urgent and grave: American grand strategy and the international order it had sustained since World War II were in jeopardy.

As we watched the forty-fifth president of the United States take his oath of office, we shared in this dire prognosis. We were, however, perplexed by the power our colleagues seemed to ascribe to this singular figure. American politics had, after all, seemed riven for some time. The country's global role was, no doubt, under increasing stress from foreign rivals, and it was ever more clear that one of the United States' antagonists had interfered in the presidential election to produce this outcome. International trade had become a domestic live wire, and the United Kingdom had just been seized by Brexit. We could not say precisely how these vectors converged in our own national convulsion. But it seemed to us that Trump was less an architect of the maelstrom than an avatar for forces that would confound American policy for years or decades.

The question was not an academic one—it had immediate implications for the strategic options Washington would face when some semblance of normalcy resumed on "the day after Trump." If President Trump was an isolated political shock, the United States could attempt to restore its global role after his departure—knowing, of course, that significant damage might occur in the interim. If he was, however, a symptom and not a cause, the prescription was far more comprehensive: American policymakers would have to devise an entirely new approach to the world, reckoning with the forces that had borne and would outlast him. Equal parts bewildered and skeptical, we began a multi-year inquiry into the fate of U.S. foreign policy: could it be restored, or had it already been ineluctably transformed?

We quickly determined that the crisis seizing American foreign policy and international order was not reducible to Trump, even though he exacerbated it. Structural transformations in the international and domestic underpinnings of American strategy began before his appearance on the national stage and will endure beyond his time in the White House. Focusing solely on the president's pronouncements, proclivities, and policies obscures these more fundamental and enduring forces at the expense of sound analysis and strategy. Undue emphasis on the president himself has real costs: this approach may leave the United States radically ill equipped to face twenty-first-century challenges.

Since the election of 2016 we have trained our attention over the horizon, looking ahead to the day after Trump, in an effort to elude that trap. Our endeavor culminated in this book: we reckon with the tectonic shifts taking place at home and abroad, and we design an American grand strategy that anticipates the world to come.

Since the end of the Cold War, the United States' unparalleled power sustained an international order—in essence, an array of norms, laws, and institutions to regulate interactions among states—predicated on liberal values and American preferences. Although this order redounded significantly to the United States' benefit, it was never destined for the permanence envisioned by "end of history" proclamations; instead, like all past orders, it reflected a transitory alignment of U.S. power and grand strategy, overlain by the patterns of interaction among states. Under pressure from global power shifts, technological change, and revolutionary domestic transformations, past orders have collapsed, most typically in the paroxysms of major wars. Today, the central task for strategists is to update the increasingly obsolete post–Cold War "liberal international order" without the cataclysm of violent conflict among great powers. Averting catastrophe necessarily requires a rejection of slavish devotion to grand strategies of yore. A new, forward-looking approach must begin by taking stock of the world as it will be one or two decades hence, rather than the world as it was in 1945, 1989, or even 2001.

At home, the United States faces the greatest threats. Geopolitical realities challenge its model of state-society relations, and the federal government has allowed the nation's technology base to become untethered from American interests and international strategy. Meanwhile, the United States is increasingly polarized by partisan animosities afflicting all dimensions of politics—including foreign policy—with chronic volatility. This unpredictability, in turn, makes it more difficult for the nation to act reliably and deliberately overseas.

Abroad, the United States faces a rapidly shifting landscape—though, in many respects, the U.S. position remains propitious. The international system is growing increasingly multipolar in character: China is rising rapidly and is already a peer competitor in Asia, Russia is declining but remains capable of revanchist disruption, and numerous emerging economies in the Indo-Pacific, led by India, will contribute to a region with diverse economic power centers. Alliances continue to redound to the United States' benefit, despite U.S. allies' demographic and economic stagnation, as allies are capable in critical domains of competition, such as the provision of economic development aid and high-technology innovation. Meanwhile, the rapid pace of technological change is reconfiguring the state-society relationships at the heart of all nations' power, and China is at the forefront of a new model of "techno-authoritarianism" that could confer considerable competitive advantages. While scholars often cite connections between international affairs and additional global or domestic trends—such as populism—this study focuses only on those trends whose connection to American strategy has been established through rigorous social science research. Policymakers must heed these forces, as each has a clear and direct causal link to American foreign policy.

Washington has lost global military primacy and will face revisionist, great-power competitors with dramatically different domestic models, conflict is likely to unfold primarily in nonmilitary domains, international cooperation will be episodic and informal, and middle powers will assume particular importance in a system defined both by U.S.-China rivalry and a multipolar diffusion of power more broadly. Though far from exhaustive, these trends represent the most consequential forces that will act upon American strategy over the next ten to fifteen years. Taken together, they suggest a future in which the United States will remain quite powerful—if it can subdue its domestic demons.

As the unipolar moment wanes, so too must any illusions of the United States' ability to craft order unilaterally and universally according to its own liberal preferences. Instead, coming decades will feature a contest over the future of international order. The emergent order will be layered and differentiated, with distinct regimes, each with different participants, for various regions and domains—though some legacy institutions will endure alongside new governing constructs. The international landscape that Washington must navigate includes a rising great power (China) and a declining one (Russia), a rapidly ascending middle power (India), and long-standing allies with highly advanced economies in the strategically vital regions of Asia (Japan, South Korea, and Australia, among others) and Europe (Germany, France, the United Kingdom, and more).

Given China's grand strategic aim of regional hegemony and its burgeoning vision of international organization, the future of the Asian regional order and global technological governance will be most hotly contested, while a highly stressed international economic order may endure if it modernizes. Russia lacks an affirmative vision for order, whether in Europe or globally, and it will likely continue a spoiling strategy, sowing disorder and aligning with China as its interests allow. As a rapidly rising nation, India will play a pivotal role in the future order. Eschewing any permanent alliances, Delhi's grand strategy seeks to forestall China's disruption of the regional order in Asia through closer cooperation with the United States and its partners, even as its developing-country status and illiberal drift may produce alignments with Beijing on climate, trade, and possibly even tech governance. As bulwarks against revisionism, allies like Japan and Germany are essential partners in twenty-first-century order building—though harmonious alignment is not assured and cooperation may rest on satisfying their demands for reform to sclerotic institutions like the UN and WTO.

For American strategists, this suite of international interactions indicates the need to differentiate between those elements of order that remain largely stable—like the UN system and its underlying norms of sovereign equality—and those that will be subject to competition between Washington and Beijing. In the latter category, coalition building will be paramount: at best, uniting with allies like Japan and Germany alongside partners like India can establish widely accepted rules and regimes; at worst, these partnerships are necessary to ensure that antithetical norms and institutions do not crystallize. Contrary to the predictions of analysts who see order exclusively through an ideological lens, the nonunitary nature of twenty-first-century order means governance will not divide neatly between authoritarian and democratic blocs. As it crafts ordering confederacies, therefore, the United States must work with mixed regimes whose interests align with America's on distinct issues, like freedom of navigation or high-standards free trade, and occasionally cooperate with illiberal rivals like Russia and China in discrete areas.

In response to these emerging realities, the United States needs a new strategic vision: the pursuit of an open international system. Drawing on its historical antecedents for inspiration and precaution, openness has several core objectives and requirements. It seeks, first and foremost, to guarantee American security and prosperity by preventing rivals from establishing closed spheres of influence, characterized by hierarchical dominance of weaker states by mightier ones. Openness therefore requires the political independence of all states, free access to the global commons of sea and space, transparent and effective international institutions, extension of open governance to new domains like technology and climate, and support for existing democracies. In employing this strategy, acting as a force for openness, the United States will focus intensively on Asia and exhibit significant restraint in the Middle East, but each region will demand a distinct balance of military, economic, diplomatic, and technological engagement. Insisting upon the United States' international leadership role but departing from reliance on primacy as the cornerstone of a messianic liberal mission, a strategy of openness departs from post–Cold War liberal universalism, Cold War–style containment, and the traditional alternative of retrenchment.

Of course, openness cannot encompass all American objectives—but it trains strategists' sights on the most important challenges. If a significant swath of Europe or Asia became closed to outside diplomacy, commerce, and military transit, American national security and prosperity would suffer grievously, with effects much greater than any other identifiable threats. For the United States, an open system is necessary but insufficient to achieve security and prosperity. Without it, Washington cannot count on the continued interdependence of nation-states required to obtain these objectives. Furthermore, the United States is the only country that can guarantee an open system. Far from neglecting transnational challenges, an openness strategy seeks cooperation with other great powers through existing institutions and novel structures where mutual interests align on issues like climate, health, and migration. Moreover, openness is a construct for international interactions and outcomes, not a domestic policy—it does not require participating states to sacrifice their borders and sovereignty, it does not encompass individual liberties, and it accepts the necessity of domestic as well as multilateral actions to mitigate the negative externalities of openness where they occur.

To act as a force for openness globally, the United States must begin by building strength at home in a number of ways. America must lay the foundation for long-term competitiveness through investments in the American people, economy, and democracy. Bridging the gap that separates the tech sector from the national interest can be achieved through significant investments in R&D alongside regulatory, legislative, and policy steps that incentivize new models of private-sector cooperation. The United States must also insulate its global strategy from the volatility wrought by partisan polarization by embedding foreign policy in a web of nonpartisan and public-private partnerships. At the same time, the United States must prepare for international competition by recognizing the extent to which it will occur outside the area of defense. Washington must therefore revitalize its moribund State Department, catalyze new heights of interagency capacity and coordination to counter threats and advance American interests in the gray zone, modernize the nation's military capabilities, exploit the promise of private-sector collaboration on intelligence and international investment, and reorient alliances and partnerships to meet the threats and seize the opportunities of the future.

Upon these pillars, Washington must craft an open order for the twenty-first century. The United States should join with allies and partners to defend free access to the global commons, especially to sea and space; pioneer an open economic order through an interlocking strategy of WTO reform, plurilateral trade agreements that can set high standards where multilateral institutions fail, and carefully tailored defenses of the most sensitive domestic technologies and industries; advance open norms for technology governance while establishing new, credible deterrence thresholds in cyberspace; construct cooperative climate, migration, and health regimes that build on the voluntary, inclusive model of the Paris Agreement; and pursue reform to the UN Security Council to enhance its legitimacy through better international representation. While every element of the openness strategy may not succeed in equal measure, and some may fail entirely, the costs of inaction are far too high to wager. If the United States fails to undertake these reforms, it will find itself with a foreign policy utterly ill equipped for the world it faces, and with diminishing means for course correction.

In making the case for a novel American grand strategy for the day after Trump, we aim to assist scholars, analysts, and policymakers as they grapple with the contours of a burgeoning era of world and domestic politics. We present original analysis of the causes and consequences of global transformations and develop a novel strategic framework for the United States. In so doing, we build synthetically on research that spans multiple disciplines, including political science, history, and area studies.

The arguments outlined in this book advance debates about the future of American grand strategy and international order by breaking free of the stale constructs that have dominated these discussions in recent decades. American internationalism depends on neither liberal universalism nor economic and military primacy; discipline and prioritization do not signal retrenchment. An openness strategy draws upon the insights of numerous foreign policy traditions, joining realists' respect for material power and its structural implications with liberals' insistence on the value of interdependence and confidence in the cooperation engendered by international institutions and regimes. Where scholars or practitioners disagree with our policy prescriptions, we nonetheless hope they will value our identification of the core strategic problem at hand.

The task before American policymakers is clear and monumental: to prepare American strategy and international order for twenty-first-century challenges that bear little resemblance to the past, while recognizing the loss of material primacy and rapidly shifting international and domestic conditions. The United States remains the world's most powerful nation with unparalleled, if not unilateral, ability to shape international politics. If American strategy can peacefully manage the order renovation demanded by tectonic shifts at home and abroad, Washington can support an open international system that keeps it and much of the world prosperous and safe. If it neglects to do so, the consequences will be grave. Without U.S. effort, forces of closure may seize technological and economic domains, as well as broad geographic areas, making it impossible for American power to penetrate, and for it to secure the cooperation and interdependence upon which it has long relied. The charge, moreover, is exigent: the United States' relative power position will diminish in the decades to come. If it fails to adopt a suitable strategy and approach to order now, the United States will find itself straining to secure its vital interests in the years ahead. The Trump presidency, far from a solution, is merely a chaotic avatar of this epochal challenge. It is time to begin preparing for the day after, so that the United States is equipped to lead the world toward an open future once the chaos breaks.

ONE

Power, Strategy, and Order

Foreign policy elites have reached a near-consensus that the liberal international order led by the United States since World War II is fraying, as its institutions, laws, and norms are growing less effective and its principles of free markets, democracy promotion, constraints on the use of force, and multilateral cooperation are becoming less entrenched. With Donald Trump's ascendance to the presidency on a platform of unpredictability, the future of international politics—and the role of American leadership therein—appeared to enter a state of flux. The world the next president inherits will differ profoundly from the international environment the United States has faced since the end of the Cold War and, in many ways, since 1945.

The term "liberal international order" has always served as a shorthand for a fairly benign form of U.S. hegemony. This order is primarily Western in its origins, and liberal preferences for free markets, international institutions, human rights, democracy, and American leadership are at its foundation. As rising social, economic, and political anxieties seem to erode domestic political support for these tenets within the United States, the pressure on American foreign policy and the international order will likely intensify. Our current moment is almost certainly not a random shock, however, but a product of political and economic forces that will outlast any one administration. Comprehending it therefore requires a strategic reckoning that both accounts for and looks beyond the present political paroxysm.

The 2016 election spawned widespread debate about the future of American strategy and international order. Strategists and scholars on both sides of the political divide declared the international order in peril in the hands of the forty-fifth president. Eminent analysts of international relations acknowledged some broader political forces, including populism, nationalism, and economic stagnation, as contributing to the decay of the U.S.-led postwar order, but they placed the lion's share of the blame on the new chief executive.[1] Others argued that the liberal international order was never as liberal, international, or orderly as the American policy narrative alleged. If the liberal international order did indeed exist, it was decidedly limited in its geographic and historical scope. This counter-narrative held that the postwar international order contained such drastic variations in its implementation across time and space that it gave no particular prescriptions for how to promote democracy, manage alliances, or craft regional postures.[2] While some thinkers have rushed to defend the core underpinnings of the liberal order as fundamentally sound, calling for more liberalism to buttress listing institutions and regimes, even these optimists acknowledge the birth of powerful forces that will fundamentally reshape postwar politics. International order is therefore under duress due to forces that defy any one theory or paradigm.[3]

Three years into this lofty debate, strategists have generally come to recognize that the country will not have the luxury of returning to foreign policy business-as-usual in 2021 or 2025.[4] The conviction that the liberal order is unraveling is relatively recent, but many of the trends that contribute to its fraying have been years in the making. Retrospectively, the 2008 financial crisis was a leading indicator of America's waning primacy—a punctuated shock that fostered the conditions for a period of competitive international relations and less functional domestic politics. The domestic and international trends that caused the United States to stumble and brought Trump to power will ensure that Washington cannot simply recoup its unipolar position atop a familiar liberal international order in a few years' time. Yet the debate over the future of American grand strategy—so long reduced to a stylized caricature between liberal internationalism and realist retrenchment— has grown musty. These discussions too often look backward, focused on relitigating post–Cold War failures rather than grappling with the domestic and international conditions Washington will face in the future—conditions with which neither pole of this false grand strategic dichotomy sufficiently reckons.[5] If strategists wish to define *how* the United States can navigate the world a new president will find, they must account for the forces that have already begun to reshape international politics and build strategies toward order accordingly.

The future of the international order is not simply the domain of esoteric strategy; it is the charge of new leadership. The powerful forces exerting pressure on American foreign policy and international relations will not abate when the current political paroxysm eases. No leader, however competent and determined, can arrest the structural trends afoot. A new chief executive cannot simply heal the damage wrought by one administration by enacting palliative policies; she or he must also devise strategies for a fast-changing world and the systems that order it. Essential to that task is an understanding of international order and its relationship to power—and why that age-old nexus has placed the United States in a moment of stunning and ineluctable change.

What Is International Order?

International order refers to the governing arrangements that establish fundamental rules and principles in international politics and settle expectations among states. In any given historical era, international order is constructed when states create these basic organizing arrangements for the system. Because they are constructed by sovereign states, these structures are by definition transitory. They can be neglected, contested, upended, and dismantled. Throughout modern history, international order has most commonly broken down through major wars. After their settlement, novel orders have been established among states based on new power configurations.[6] Scholars therefore associate major changes to international order with hegemonic violence.

When they are formed, international orders may vary along a number of dimensions. One is functional scope, or what domains the order governs. For example, orders can be formed exclusively around the idea of sovereignty and security protection, as in the Westphalian order in Europe, or they can be expansive, governing economic, social, political, and other aspects of interstate relations, as in the post–World War II order. Orders can be highly institutionalized—organized into formal and informal regimes, rules, and routines—as in the post–World War II global order or the East Asian tribute system. They can also exist simply on the basis of a convergence of state interests, the case with the Concert of Europe, or on top-down hegemonic coercion, as with the Ottoman or Spanish Empires. Within a given order, power can be centralized or decentralized and may be organized around different configurations of power: multipolar, bipolar, or unipolar. International orders can also operate with varying degrees of hierarchy, functioning among sovereign equals—like the UN system, which nevertheless carved out a special status for the World War II victors on the Security Council—or based on hegemonic control, as in imperial orders. These dimensions create a range of possible orders.[7]

A final order characteristic is geographic scope: orders can be global, encompassing most or all of the states in the international system, or they can be regional, limited to a particular region or sub-region. Many historical "international" orders have actually been regional orders, involving one continent—as in the Westphalian system or the Congress of Vienna in Europe. Contemporary order is therefore not a single structure at all.[8] The modern-day international order is fairly thick, comprising myriad political, security, and economic governance regimes and institutions, while regional orders have in many ways become secondary, engaging geographically bounded issue areas that cannot be addressed universally or globally. The European Union (EU) and Association of Southeast Asian Nations (ASEAN), for example, deal with integration at the regional level, but do not supersede activities of their member states in the World Bank and the UN.

During the Cold War, order functioned in layers. The UN system was constructed well before the superpower standoff crystallized, with the aim of governing the political, security, and economic relations of its sovereign members.[9] Once the chilly deadlock took hold, however, the United States and the Soviet Union created other institutions, such as their dueling alliance blocs; still other regional organizations were born in Asia, Africa, and Latin America only after decolonization. A future order might, therefore, have international, universal elements that deal with arms control, climate change, and the global economy, with regional security orders that are increasingly organized around the United States and China.[10]

As a conceptual lens, international order elucidates the interrelationship between power, strategy, and governance. That any given order rests upon the power configurations of the era is undeniable. State power derives from the capabilities or resources it can use to influence global outcomes.[11] Although military assets have historically been primary in geopolitics, the sources of influence may be economic, social, cultural, or technological, and their most relevant manifestations vary across time. The prevailing distribution of these endowments—military and economic capabilities chief among them—has generally determined which powers will manage international governance, whatever form it may take. Yet an international system's material attributes do not solely dictate the grand strategies of its leading states. Instead, major powers formulate grand strategies on the basis of a suite of domestic as well as international factors— such as domestic politics, state-society relations, strategic culture, ideology, geography, and individual leadership—that translate into a vision for how international order can advance national interests. The organizing principles of a given order thus reflect great powers' preferences, and may even allow them to occasionally flout prevailing rules and norms by virtue of superior position.[12]

Yet even as international orders rely on the power and coercive backing of leading states, they are not simply reducible to the will of great powers. Once rules, regimes, and institutions coalesce, they assume potency of their own, reducing the costs and increasing the benefits of international political interactions. Even at the peak of American power, for example, the liberal international order censured untoward U.S. behavior, though it could not thwart it entirely. Orders create some sense of predictability which, in turn, encourages states to perpetuate prevailing rules and norms through dense patterns of international interactions that have generally increased stability and fostered cooperation over time. This tight relationship between international power, strategy, and governance has profound implications: if the leading state's power is transformed in significant ways, the international organizations, regimes, and rules that have rested upon it will likely also change.

Power and Order through History
Orders have existed throughout history in various forms, and typically transform when underlying power distributions shift. War is the most frequent mechanism for international order turnover.[13] As

scholar John Ikenberry notes, the major transitions in world order have come after the settlement of "hegemonic wars": 1648, 1713, 1815, 1919, and 1945 are some of the iconic order-building moments. Empires, another form of order, have also risen and fallen throughout history—the Romans and Greeks, Ottomans, Mongols, and others shaped the territory they controlled in their image and to suit their interests, but often faltered in the face of invasion and violence.[14]

One prominent example of international order, the Peace of Westphalia, which ended the Thirty Years' War in 1648, continues to define geopolitics. The Treaty of Westphalia codified the notion of state sovereignty; the central objective of creating such an order was to counter the threat of Catholic and imperial hegemony.[15] In the treaty's declaration that the Holy Roman emperor could not impose Catholicism at will on principalities and could have no say in their dynastic politics, the idea of the independence of states from one another and from a central governing force emerged. This ordering principle has been dominant in the international system ever since.[16]

The Westphalian international order was a thin and narrow one—it conceived of order based on sovereignty alone and covered just the European continent. In this sense, it was in fact a small regional order; the order was informal in that it had no institutions or other mechanisms for enforcing its norms. The Westphalian order also legitimized the use of war to settle disputes—war was proscribed only if used as a tool to alter the 1648 settlement.[17] The peace stabilized the fractious European continent for nearly two hundred years, but ultimately broke down due to shifts in the balance of power. The French Revolution and rise of Napoleon led to fifteen years of continental conflict. Diplomats who gathered in Vienna in 1815 to negotiate the peace with France were determined to prevent another bid for European hegemony capable of dramatically upsetting continental stability.[18]

At the Congress of Vienna, the allied powers established a new ordering principle for Europe: the balance of power, or the notion that no great power should undertake to conquer so much territory that it gained a material advantage over the other great powers. If one did so, the other great powers in the system would combine to check the hegemonic ambitions of the wayward member. The balance of power was not an automatic feature of the system; it was thought of as a "diplomatic creation that required constant monitoring and managing."[19] This principle gave rise to the Concert of Europe, an informal institution that involved "frequent high-level diplomatic consultation among representatives of the major powers."[20] Unlike Westphalia, the peace signed in Paris and Vienna entailed a system of active management and commitments to undertake joint actions against disturbances of the peace in Europe.

The concert began to suffer almost immediately due to disagreements about how to manage the ideal balance. High-level diplomacy lasted only until 1822. The Vienna concert had never agreed on the events that would trigger collective action to punish an aggressor. Austria, Prussia, Russia, and Bourbon France regarded "any revolution, anywhere" as sufficient grounds for collective action. Great Britain disagreed, arguing that only *"external aggression* by a revolutionary power" called for intervention.[21] Eventually, the rise of a united Germany caused the destruction of the Concert of Europe by 1871.[22]

Regional orders have, of course, existed outside of Europe. In East Asia, states created a thick order based on the hierarchical tribute system. Like the orders in Europe, the tribute system arose from conflict, including the disintegration of centralized control over China, the Mongol invasions, and persistent regional strife.[23] By the late 1300s, however, China was stable enough to establish a multinational system of control within East Asia—a Confucian regional order. A defining feature of the tribute system was the presumption of inequality. China sat atop a regional hierarchy, and other states were ranked based on their cultural similarity to China; regardless of status, they all were required to demonstrate their inferiority and deference to China.[24]

On the basis of cultural hierarchy, as well as ongoing bargaining with subordinate states, this Sino-centric order regulated regional trade through its governance of "tribute missions."[25] The system kept the peace in East Asia for a remarkably long period of time. From 1368 to 1841, there were only two major interstate wars, one between Vietnam and China (1407–28) and another between Japan and Korea (1592–98). The lasting peace was in no small part due to China's implicit commitment not to use its dominance exploitatively, thereby purchasing some legitimacy from surrounding states. As a result, the system managed borders, dealt with crises, and regulated a host of interactions beyond trade. The tribute system collapsed with the arrival of European powers in Asia. When Great Britain defeated China in the Opium Wars and European powers scrambled to create spheres of influence within China, the prevailing regional notions of hierarchy and status were upended. China lost its leadership position in Asia and with it, by 1841, the order it had created.[26]

The Post–World War II International Order

Following World War I, Woodrow Wilson's Fourteen Points, the Washington Naval Conference of 1920–21, the League of Nations, and the Geneva Convention of 1929 represented early attempts to conjure a truly thick, international, and philosophically liberal form of order.[27] The war had shattered the legitimacy of an order based on the balance of power, and rigorous governing principles and institutions seemed necessary. In particular, Wilson envisioned a liberal world order that would base international politics around the principles of free trade, sovereignty, territorial integrity, and the peaceful resolution of disputes.[28] His Republican counterparts in the U.S. Senate did not agree that American security and prosperity required commitments nearly so broad, however, and feared that the league would instead entangle the country in European affairs.

Apart from American nonparticipation, the League of Nations was fatally flawed because it relied on self-regulation to operate. The territorial integrity of members and the requirement that all nations submit their disputes to the league for arbitration rested merely on the pledge that members would do so, not on any binding commitment. As a result, the league did not really outlaw war so much as it served as a means for voluntary dispute resolution.[29] Further, the system failed to incorporate Germany while saddling it with onerous postwar reparations, creating an environment in which militant nationalism could flourish.[30] These flaws rendered the system ill equipped to manage the rise of fascism and the Great Depression.

The outbreak of World War II upended this incipient liberal system. Prior to the defeat of Nazi Germany, the United States and Great Britain had begun to lead the way toward the formation of a new world order, one far more ambitious than orders of the past, that was retrospectively termed the "liberal international order." At its core sat the United Nations and its institutions, which retained universal membership throughout the Cold War and were founded on the basis of sovereign equality. For the United States, the new system was a pragmatic pursuit: it sought to secure its prosperity and its national security with rules and institutions that could prevent the next Great Depression and world war. Indeed, Washington had come to believe that its interests could not otherwise be secured.

But as the superpower standoff took root, another layer of order bifurcated between Western-style democracies and the Communist world. The liberal order focused on cooperative security, open markets, multilateral governance, and American hegemonic leadership; it found form in the Bretton Woods financial institutions, the North Atlantic Treaty Organization (NATO), and later the EU

(European Union) and the World Trade Organization (WTO).[31]
The Communist world had its own organizations and rules, including the Comintern and Comecon; the Soviets also had a rival to
NATO in the Warsaw Pact alliance system. And while this second
layer of principle-based order entailed significant competition between the superpowers, it also bounded conflict and effectively
codified spheres of geopolitical influence. The Cold War was,
therefore, highly ordered, if split in its organization.[32]

While many of the ordering principles foundational to the liberal international order far predated 1945, they seeded a new set of
postwar international institutions and norms with political, security, and economic dimensions. This order was far from a single,
crystalline structure that emerged fully formed from the ashes of
World War II, however; it was cobbled together over the course
of the twentieth century in striated layers.[33] Conjured as a largely
Western vision, the order diffused into Asia, Africa, and Latin
America following decolonization, often with problematic consequences for those regions. It cracked and listed in the economic
stagnation of the 1970s as the Bretton Woods institutions appeared
to be in abject decline. Indeed, liberal order claimed universalism
only with the demise of the Soviet Union and apparent triumph of
the liberal system in the early 1990s. The term "liberal international order" is therefore something of a misnomer—the system
to which it refers was never wholly liberal, truly international, or
entirely orderly.[34] Further, it is hardly the only form of order that is
possible. Despite its limitations, however, the postwar order has
largely boasted a propitious record.

The Record of the Liberal International Order

The liberal world order has produced numerous political benefits
for the United States and the international system. This order also
helped manage the world through significant political transitions,
surviving through epochal shifts that might otherwise have led to

chaos. Between 1945 and 2019, the number of sovereign states grew from 86 to 196, and the order evolved with them, expanding its scope and reach. The extension of the order following decolonization, as with the creation of new regional institutions like ASEAN and the African Union (AU), and the incorporation of former Soviet states at the end of the Cold War proceeded smoothly for the most part. The order has also encouraged the spread of democracy through support for regime transitions, foreign aid, socialization in international organizations, and the force of liberal norms. In 1945, 29 percent of the world's countries were democratic; today 57 percent are.[35] In 1945, only 11 percent of the world's population lived in a democracy, compared with 56 percent in 2015. From a security perspective, the increase in the number of democracies has led to a more peaceful international environment because of the well-established tendency of democratic states to avoid war with each other.[36]

The liberal international order has crafted a generally prosperous and open international economy, which has delivered benefits even if the gains have been unevenly distributed. The world is experiencing unprecedented economic growth; in the last generation alone, the value of yearly global economic production has doubled. The institutionalization of free trade under the General Agreement on Tariff and Trade (GATT) / WTO process produced estimated global income gains of $510 billion between 1995 and 2011.[37] Very few countries in the world experienced negative economic growth between 1960 and 2016, and most of these were conflict-affected states, including the Democratic Republic of the Congo and the Central African Republic. Assisting the general growth, levels of foreign aid have continued to rise in absolute terms (helped along by increasing contributions from non-Western states like China and Brazil).[38]

Much of the world has benefited from these gains. The average global GDP per capita moved from $3,277 in 1950 to $14,574 in

2016. The proportion of the world's citizens living in extreme poverty diminished from 36 percent in 1990 to 9.9 percent in 2015, and the World Bank estimates that this trend of poverty reduction will continue.[39] The growth in the global economy has significantly helped the population of developing countries; in India, China, Ghana, Ethiopia, and Indonesia (countries where half the population lived in poverty a generation ago), extreme poverty reduced by more than 50 percent in the last two decades. These gains are not only financial; public health has also undergone a massive improvement. In 1970, the global rate of child mortality (the deaths of children under five years of age per 1,000 children) was 141, while in 2010 it was only 57. Likewise, global life expectancy has risen dramatically—from fifty-nine years in 1970 to seventy years in 2012.[40]

Security has also improved, abetting these humanitarian gains. In a sharp break with history, there has been no war between major powers since 1945. This "long peace" probably has multiple causes, including the presence of nuclear weapons and economic interdependence, but it is highly likely that a major contributing factor is the rules and regimes that have increased the costs of interstate violence while reducing the benefits of territorial conquest. By entrenching political, security, and economic cooperation in unprecedentedly formal ways, this order has, over time, shifted incentives against interstate war.[41] Globally, interstate violence is at a historic nadir, and although several geopolitically salient international territorial disputes endure (the South China Sea, Kashmir, Crimea), new territorial claims are rare. Moreover, when conquest has occurred in flagrant violation of the UN Charter, as in Korea or the 1991 Gulf War, internationally sanctioned efforts to restore the peace have largely succeeded.[42]

Of course, the liberal international order's record is far from perfect. The underlying aspiration toward liberal universalism often collided with the difficulty of democracy promotion in authoritarian societies, and efforts to promote regime change through military intervention exacted immense costs in blood and treasure. Liberal order also contains fundamental tensions between its foundational principle of state sovereignty and its grander aspirations of ideological diffusion. And, as the United States has proven on multiple occasions, there are fundamental limits on the extent to which order can bind the most powerful states.[43] A considerable expectations gap has also emerged within the system. The liberal order's promises of peace and prosperity went unrequited in many regions where penetration was uneven, and passed over specific countries and populations. Globalization, for example, has benefited the world writ large but produced uneven gains within states, including in liberal democracies. Despite the absence of great-power conflicts, there have been plenty of civil wars, and the system has not averted significant economic crises. Finally, the liberal world order has often been too vague a concept to provide specific policy prescriptions. A "rules-based" international order may indeed exist, but the manifestation of these rules is underspecified for any given global problem.[44]

Moreover, twenty-first-century challenges have laid bare some glaring gaps in order, revealing the fact that some of the United States' greatest strategic concerns may not be subject to rules or institutions at all. Climate change remains basically ungoverned, save on a strictly voluntary basis. Emerging technologies and domains, ranging from cyberspace to artificial intelligence and biotechnology, feature few to no rules of the road. While UN conflict-prevention laws and institutions have been effective over time, the strength of these norms may have helped to encourage would-be challengers to embrace coercion that occurs below traditional conflict thresholds, like China's island construction in the South China Sea or Russian cyber interference in foreign elections, as this "gray zone" between peace and war occupies ungoverned space. If the United States and like-minded partners were to remake international order from scratch today, it would almost certainly depart from the rules, structures, and scope of its successful postwar predecessor.

The Order Will Not Endure

Some thinkers of a liberal orientation argue that international order remains on a firm footing. According to this narrative, the United States does not face meaningful decline, and therefore need only recommit to the order to fortify it.[45] Other liberal internationalists argue that liberal values continue to have universal appeal and therefore will endure despite autocratic challengers, or that like-minded middle powers can buttress the prevailing order to prevent its collapse.[46] In each of these accounts, restoration is possible and desirable.

Yet these perspectives miss an uncomfortable truth: transformative forces have already fundamentally altered the context that produced and sustained the liberal international order. Geopolitical, technological, economic, and sociopolitical changes will extend far beyond the discrete shock of the Trump presidency and illuminate a world in which central elements of the liberal international order are no longer sustainable. Indeed, rather than liberalizing themselves in the order's image, as many post–Cold War optimists had hoped, Russia and China are demanding a modified order that better accommodates the ambitions and appetites of their domestic regimes.[47] Already ensconced within the liberal order, dissatisfied illiberal powers will continue to challenge and undermine it through variegated strategies of revisionism. Any model of future order that does not contend with these realities cannot endure.

Order transformation is not, however, a simple matter of translating changed power balances into new governing arrangements. Typically, such change has followed major war. Yet the confluence of the nuclear revolution, deep economic interdependence, and unprecedented institutionalization renders war a tremendously costly mechanism for change and places a particular premium on identifying avenues for peaceful order transformation. If hegemonic war is less likely than it was in the past, and the United States continues to retain a favorable global position, it follows that Washington has an opportunity to preemptively revise its strategy for international order to put the system on firmer foundations for the future. Such modifications could fortify some elements of the extant order against emerging challengers while creating new, selective, and differentiated arrangements to help the United States, its allies, and its partners compete where universalist approaches fall short.

Yet the precise contours of this strategy are far from obvious. While structural pressures may shape the United States' range of grand strategic options, they will not determine its path—as the robustness of the debate over the future of America's global role amply demonstrates. Just as the liberal international order construct emerged because the United States elected to pursue liberal internationalism over its alternatives at several critical twentieth-century junctures, twenty-first-century order will depend on Washington's strategic choices in the coming years.

Moreover, the range of these choices is wider and more diverse than the well-worn grand strategy debate between retrenchment and liberal hegemony would typically suggest. Skeptical of the very concept of international order, advocates of retrenchment ascribe little value to strategies designed to shape and defend it. This position reflects a fundamental rejection of the assumption that national security requires the United States to police a world order amenable to American values, institutions, and economic penetration.[48] As the scholars John Mearsheimer and Stephen Walt argue: "By pursuing a strategy of 'offshore balancing,' Washington would forgo ambitious efforts to remake other societies and concentrate on what really matters: preserving U.S. dominance in the Western Hemisphere and countering potential hegemons in Europe, Northeast Asia, and the Persian Gulf."[49] But even in forestalling the rise of a Eurasian hegemon, the first line of defense would be regional powers, and the United States would intervene only if absolutely necessary. Offshore balancers differ in their approaches to nuclear proliferation and counterterrorism, but overall they agree that the rewards of pulling back from global engagement will outweigh the risks.

Those who favor liberal hegemony, by contrast, argue that the United States should stay the course—their preferred grand strategy is "the devil we know." While distinct from the liberal international order, grand strategies oriented around using American power to entrench and extend liberalism have undergirded the order since its inception. Proponents of this approach identify the post–World War II order's liberal character as fundamental to its success, citing the past seven decades of peace and prosperity as a marked departure from the "economic mercantilism, political conflict, and repeated war" that previously characterized much of world history.[50] Even in the unipolar moment, "American strategy has played a central role in making the post–Cold War international system more stable, more liberal, and more favorable to U.S. interests and ideals than it would otherwise have been." Many such advocates see primacy as both feasible and necessary to mount a robust defense of the liberal international order—contending either that primacy persists, or that it can be recaptured through significant defense investments.[51]

Of course, considerable nuance exists in the grand strategies advanced across each of these camps and those that fall outside them.[52] But too often Washington's way forward is framed in terms of a stark choice between liberal internationalism as it has been practiced since the end of the Cold War and dramatic retrenchment. To succumb to this unhelpful binary is to neglect the possibility of a more disciplined, less costly strategic pathway that nevertheless preserves the United States' ability to shape the future of international order through persistent global engagement. Furthermore, it obscures the possibility of an American strategy that promotes openness—free access to the global commons, economic exchange, information flow, and security cooperation—without insisting upon the spread of liberal domestic governance as a prerequisite.

For policymakers, this opportunity is fleeting but of tremendous historic importance. If the United States can chart a strategic course for the novel organization of international politics, that order will bear its unmistakable imprint; it will be maximally conducive to the search for prosperity and security that led Washington to embrace postwar order in the first place. With the passage of time, however, the opportunity will wane. As international power diffuses, the United States will have diminished relative influence over the rules and regimes of the future. And regardless of whether the United States chooses to act, those new forms of order will come into being. If Washington declines the current charge, the next era of order will not just be less beneficial—it may even imperil some of the country's dearest interests.

Of course, even under optimal domestic conditions, decisions made in Washington cannot unilaterally remake international order. Amid military, economic, and political power shifts, accompanied by technological diffusion, American grand strategy will not be as determinative of international order as it was during the post–World War II or post–Cold War periods. Any successful U.S. strategy must account for the iterative and interactive bargaining process that peaceful order change must entail as the United States cooperates and competes with other important global actors—China, Russia, India, Japan, and Germany chief among them. Scholars and policymakers thus have a multifaceted mandate: they must map the forces that are likely to transform American foreign policy and international order, seek to understand other major powers' likely strategies, and design an American approach that rebuilds a favorable order amid tectonic geopolitical shifts.

Domestic Disruptions

The United States' domestic environment and choices will determine, in no small part, the world it confronts in ten to fifteen years'
time. During the post–Cold War period, the United States pos-
sessed ample resources and faced a historically propitious external
environment. Meaningful "guns versus butter" tradeoffs were rare.
As a result, policymakers encountered few domestic constraints as
they made foreign policy. Among its many harbingers, however,
the 2016 election struck scholars and commentators alike as an indication that foreign policy had come unglued from the realities of
the domestic polity. Foreign policy elites had to reconnect with and
be more responsive to domestic variables and preferences as they
grappled with the future of America's role in the world.[1]

At a moment of tectonic political change, however, it is not readily apparent which domestic trends matter for foreign policy—
or how and why they do. Venerable thinkers have posited close
relationships between foreign policy and economic dislocation,
cultural grievances linked to immigration, and income inequality,
arguing that any sustainable American strategy must respond to

these forces.[2] Yet despite their intrinsic significance, these domestic tides do not necessarily portend specific or ineluctable shifts in foreign policy. The connection between each of these variables and the world Washington will face in 2030 is, at best, unclear.

There are two major and identifiable domestic trends—the United States' ability to harness its own technological capacity and endemic political polarization—that can change the content of foreign policy and the process by which it is made, fundamentally transforming America's role in the world. Over the course of several decades, the federal government has underinvested in basic science and technology, leading to a dealignment of incentives between the private and public sectors on national security issues. Similarly, political polarization has slowly sorted the country's leadership and citizenry into oppositional blocs in ways that may significantly hamper Washington's credibility as an ally and a competitor. Polarization may amplify the effects of several other domestic issues, including alarm over the national debt, shifts in preferences due to income inequality, public opinion on specific foreign policy topics, and foreign interference in American democratic processes. By restructuring the American media and political environment into hyper-charged, bifurcated camps, polarization makes it more likely that each of these issues will have exaggerated impact on the future of foreign policy. Unless American strategy addresses each of these pernicious forces, it will be far less effective in securing U.S. interests than the country's still-formidable power should allow.

Harnessing Technological Capacity

As technological change and its diffusion refashion geopolitics, the United States' ability to harness its technology sector to its national competitive advantage—particularly on matters of foreign policy and national security—will be central to its long-term global competitiveness and ability to prevail over authoritarian challengers.

Because of problematic incentive structures in the United States, however, the U.S. government and the American technology sector have become misaligned. If this chasm widens, it may leave Washington systematically unable to leverage the U.S. technological base for national advantage, a prospect that will be devastating to the country's international position.

Historically, the U.S. government has played an instrumental role in funding cutting-edge research—particularly in areas that address vital national interests but may not be commercially viable. During the Cold War, the federal government considered research and development (R&D) spending an investment in national security; outlays peaked at above 2 percent of GDP in the 1970s. In the post–Cold War world, such spending atrophied significantly, falling from just over 1 percent of GDP in 2001 to 0.7 percent of GDP in 2018.[3] It is now at a historical nadir. Today, the United States ranks tenth globally in government R&D investments, and this position continues to erode. Consequently, the private sector has become the largest funder of both applied and basic R&D; in 2015, the federal government furnished less than half of all funding for basic research for the first time since World War II. By neglecting its critical role as an investor in basic science and technology, the U.S. government left the private sector to chart its own course.[4]

With less government investment in both material and political terms, American industry—in particular the tech sector—has pursued its own interests. Absent any mandate to addresses national security requirements, Silicon Valley has naturally sought to protect access to the foreign markets necessary for future growth, including the ability to work in emerging populous markets. Asia, for example, contains nearly half of the world's population, but its market is only 55 percent internet-penetrated, meaning that an enormous quantity of people remain to be connected.[5] That pull to untapped foreign markets will remain strong. This opportunity, in turn, creates disincentives for American technology companies to appear as government partners in U.S. national security—instead they wish to maintain the purported political and value neutrality of their platforms.

This lack of unified mission has also led to a lamentable absence of technological expertise in government, particularly in the national security space. The yawning gap between government and Silicon Valley salaries dissuades top science, technology, engineering, and math (STEM) talent from serving in national security roles, while the pull toward opportunities to work with cutting-edge private-sector technology creates even greater distance. Government efforts to socialize the two communities, such as the Technology Fellows program, Defense Innovation Unit (DIU), and even high-level Silicon Valley visits from the president and secretary of defense, are simply not equal to the problem.[6] As a result, the government is deprived of top technology talent, including the expertise required to make and evaluate sound technology policy. Congress's lack of familiarity with ubiquitous platforms, such as Facebook, demonstrably hindered its oversight responsibility with respect to Russia's election interference—a politically devastating dalliance, to be sure, but one that was, by most accounts, not particularly sophisticated.[7] The U.S. government will need tech-literate leadership at the highest levels if it is to defend against technologically enabled threats, use technology to advance national security, and lead in the construction of new forms of international technology governance.

The gulf between national security and industry missions produces further misalignments—notably, between federal contracting processes and technological innovation. Defense contracting is a slow and highly bureaucratic process, making it difficult and risky for smaller start-ups to participate. Tech companies are rightly focused on the speed and scale of their product's adoption. The defense contracting process, however, can entail years-long delays before smaller tech firms see a profit, making collaborative ventures with government prohibitively perilous.[8] In fact, companies that receive grants from the Pentagon tend to grow at slower rates than those that do not—perhaps because firms become mired in the thicket of federal contracting regulations, which often produce suboptimal project outcomes. According to one study, 94 percent of large federal technology programs were eventually deemed unsuccessful. More than half were over budget, delayed, or did not meet user expectations.[9] Tech firms that are considering working with the federal government must therefore consider how a lumbering process may delay the benefits of the partnership and come with additional risks that other markets simply do not pose.

Analysts often focus on the cultural disconnect between Washington and Silicon Valley, and while one certainly exists, it is most likely a symptom of the public/private-sector uncoupling described here rather than a cause. The relative novelty of the tech sector—unlike, say, the aerospace industry—means it has matured in an environment of historically low federal R&D. With paltry federal investment of political or material capital and in the absence of a shared mandate, the tech workforce has become ever more suspicious of national security–related projects. Amid employee backlash, for example, Google elected not to renew an artificial intelligence–related contract with the Department of Defense, and an array of tech companies have signed a "Lethal Autonomous Weapons Pledge," committing to "neither participate in nor support the development, manufacture, trade, or use of lethal autonomous weapons."[10] These tensions also include ongoing disputes over governmental access to encrypted data.[11] Unmoored from Washington, the tech sector has flourished as a culture that self-regards as supranational, making it more skeptical still of cooperation with Washington.

With a Washington–Silicon Valley chasm already manifest, regulation may further exacerbate tensions between the government and the tech sector. Lawmakers are increasingly united behind a call for stringent privacy legislation, and the tech community appears supportive, in no small part because it prefers modest federal regulation to a labyrinth of state laws.[12] Regulatory rationalization notwithstanding, however, major tech companies will retain the desire to husband global user data and have little incentive to share it with the government. Beyond privacy laws, Washington lacks regulatory and policymaking models that are appropriate for dual-use commercial technologies.[13] Unless the tech sector works with Washington to craft and implement appropriate frameworks, relations are likely to sour further. Thus, as an unhappy consequence of its own disinvestment, and the subsequent uncoupling of tech-government incentives, the United States' ability to harness its world-leading tech innovation base for national security purposes may be in jeopardy. A failure to address these widening disconnects may mean the United States does not develop critical national security technologies and fails to adopt necessary commercial technologies with national security and foreign policy applications. Put simply, Washington may retain a cutting-edge technological base that is nonetheless incapable of serving its geopolitical ends.

Political Polarization

Political polarization may have even more grievous effects on foreign policy. The share of Americans who express consistently conservative or consistently liberal opinions has doubled over the past two decades, from 10 percent to 21 percent. This trend demonstrably applies to foreign policy: whereas public opinion studies in the early Cold War showed limited correlation between domestic and foreign policy views, greater partisan consistency began to emerge around the time of the Vietnam War.[14] A similar pattern emerges in congressional voting, as Republicans and Democrats have diverged on policy issues and centrist legislators have all but disappeared. Some research indicates that polarization is an asymmetric phenomenon, most marked on the conservative side of the political spectrum.[15] In this telling, the Republican Party has moved farther to the right than the Democratic Party has moved to the left, leading to lopsided "procedural belligerence, and indifference to the policy preferences of the wider American electorate."[16] Intransigence and ideological divergence born of hyper-partisanship manifest starkly in congressional dysfunction and gridlock on a wide range of policy priorities. Exacerbating this trend is the growth in "affective polarization," whereby negative attitudes toward members of the opposing political party have increased: the percentage of partisans who express very unfavorable opinions of the other side has doubled in the last twenty years. This "negative partisanship" makes compromise unpalatable to legislators and voters alike.[17] Polarization thus suffuses the American political process at every level.

Polarization creates a troubling demand for segmented information flows. Among elites, think tanks that espouse extreme or very specific points of view have proliferated in response to demand for more partisan policy analysis.[18] When legislators and their staffers are able to confirm and legitimize more extreme positions with think tank–promoted research, this may lead to foreign policies that are increasingly extreme; via this feedback loop, fringe views become normalized. The result is a tragically self-perpetuating cycle whereby polarized information sources lead to further policy polarization—with trickle-down effects on the mass public. Low-information voters tend to adopt elite attitudes without critical examination, particularly on foreign policy.[19] When elites are highly polarized, this leads to more mass polarization among American citizens.

Media polarization, exemplified by the explosion of partisan television channels and websites, further amplifies elite and mass polarization. The effects are not limited to hyper-partisan fanatics— even "regular" news consumers encounter more polarized media than they did in the past. Self-sorting makes matters worse, as highly differentiated news sources across the ideological spectrum allow individuals to "opt in" only to news that confirms their pre-existing beliefs.[20] The rise of new media exacerbates these trends, as social media have created a new class of media elites whose knowledge and insight do not correlate with the virality of their opinion content. These new cognoscenti have at least partially displaced expert analysts and traditional media sources as the source of "elite cues" Americans use to interpret current events.[21]

This multifaceted political polarization may undermine American strategic effectiveness through multiple channels. It militates against decisive action—particularly on the riskiest and most important decisions—resulting in suboptimal policies designed to satisfy both parties in Congress, disadvantageous delays in policy decisions or implementation, or strategically detrimental inaction.[22] This dynamic hinders national security policy as well as the effectiveness of legislative action on domestic issues with foreign policy consequences, such as tech-sector regulation. Whereas global leadership requires consistency and predictability, polarization creates the risk of dramatic swings in foreign policy when administrations change hands from Republicans to Democrats and vice versa. Legislative polarization only magnifies this effect by encouraging unilateral executive action to circumvent congressional gridlock. What is more, polarization permits major-party candidates to advocate irresponsible foreign policy positions—whether for ideological, political, or personal reasons—without concerns about recourse from their base, as strong party identity makes voters unlikely to defect from a partisan coalition even in the face of egregious misjudgment.

Deepening political polarization may have significant and pernicious consequences for U.S. foreign policy. As media and information environments become ever more segmented, bipartisan foreign policy consensus may become more elusive, as legislators lack a common set of facts. Polarization may simultaneously hamper decisive foreign policy action when it is needed and cause dramatic substantive and procedural swings when administrations change hands. In political science terms, these tendencies may, in turn, undermine the United States' ability to send credible signals to allies and adversaries alike. Both will assume that promises and threats are valid only until the administration changes, which may undermine alliances, deterrence, and multilateral agreements.[23] If foreign policy is simply a proxy for politics, the content of the United States' international commitments becomes all but meaningless.

Polarization, Cultural Grievances, and Income Inequality
Political polarization acts directly on the content and process of American foreign policy, but it may also have significant indirect effects. By making agreements harder to form and sustain, by pushing decision makers to the more extreme wings of their parties, and by making domestic fissures abundantly clear to foreign adversaries, polarization will also magnify the effects of other domestic and international trends.

Since the 2016 election, scholarship has emphasized cultural identity and income inequality as sociocultural domestic trends that may profoundly shape public opinion, including on foreign policy issues. Our research, however, has found polarization to be the dominant trend. Leading analysts have argued that long-term, immigration-induced demographic changes have led to a resurgence of nationalism and rejection of internationalism.[24] Yet cultural grievance dynamics do not appear to produce structural or generalizable trends in public opinion, particularly as they relate to foreign policy. Insofar as cultural variables did matter in the last election, they were refracted through the lens of partisanship. Similarly, no seamless link has been established between income inequality and populist movements.[25]

Domestic income inequality may, however, relate to foreign policy preferences when it acts through the intervening variable of political polarization. National income inequality is the share of all income in a country that is concentrated in the top decile or percentile of earners. The wider earnings are dispersed, the more unequal they are, and income inequality has decidedly been rising in the United States. This mounting inequality could have long-run generational effects: when parents have a lower income, their children have fewer opportunities, with less upward mobility. The compounding effects of this phenomenon imply an exponential increase in inequality across generations.[26] If the problem is not addressed through education reform and efforts to prepare young people for a changing, automation-based economy, then increasing income inequality—potentially exacerbated by massive unemployment—is likely to become an untenable economic reality.

Income inequality is deeply intertwined with partisan polarization.[27] In assessing polarization's causes, political scientists have found a tangle of variables, including inequality, immigration, and party politics, which interact through mechanisms that are complicated and multidirectional. Of all these variables, inequality and polarization appear nearly inextricable; they fell in parallel from the early 1910s to the mid-1950s, then sharply rose together from the 1970s onward.[28] Recent research suggests that income inequality's impact on polarization may be a cyclical, self-reinforcing process. In states with high income inequality, for example, legislatures have moved farther to the right on the political spectrum, as moderate Democratic leaders are replaced with Republicans. This rightward shift decreases the chances that these bodies will pass redistributive policies to ameliorate income inequality while also exacerbating polarization overall, which increases gridlock and reduces the chance that the legislatures could respond to increases in income inequality even in circumstances in which they might otherwise do so.[29] According to this causal pathway, income inequality may be both an antecedent and an amplifier of political polarization, heightening it and the ill effects it may have on American foreign policy process and content.

Polarization and Public Opinion

Although many analysts have questioned the depth of public support for American internationalism, public opinion data belie their doubts: since 2016, support for U.S. global engagement has actually increased. As of 2019, despite widening partisan divisions on specific issues, surveys show that solid majorities of Democrats, Republicans, and independents all endorse an active U.S. role in the world, and overall enthusiasm for international trade has reached unprecedented heights.[30] Yet the independent causal effect of public opinion itself on foreign policy remains indirect and difficult to establish. For example, despite its galvanizing effect on many voters, the implications of populism for American foreign policy are indeterminate. As a trend, the sources of populism are multitudinous and difficult to identify; moreover, its salience on the right and left of the political spectrum demonstrates the wide range of foreign policies that populists might support.[31] Going forward, public sentiments are unlikely to directly constrain the United States' strategic choices—instead, they are likely to be refracted through the lens of partisanship.

Nonetheless, public opinion in certain discrete areas, such as anti-trade sentiment, could alter the nation's strategic course—especially if those who hold these opinions are concentrated geographically in electorally consequential locales. Some research has suggested that automation-affected voters will prefer policy platforms focused on domestic job creation, including through more protectionist trade policies. As automation spreads, the argument goes, so too will anti-trade sentiment. Such connections require caution. The effect of automation on the U.S. labor force remains quite uncertain and anti-trade sentiments are unlikely to result in a wholesale lurch away from internationalism.[32] If these sentiments continue to flourish in a highly polarized political environment, however, they may incentivize political candidates to take more protectionist positions which, in turn, constrain their policy options once they are in power. Polarization may once again act as an intervening variable, translating specific changes in public opinion into distinct foreign policy shifts.

Polarization, Federal Spending, and the Debt

For the last several decades, budget deficits have increased, financed by massive foreign government purchases of U.S. securities. Though temporarily kept at bay by low interest rates following the 2008 financial crisis, chronic budget deficits have historically precipitated crises as interest payments claim an increasing percentage of available budget revenues. Publicly held debt is now set to double in the next decade, and the deficit will be approximately 5 percent of GDP annually in the 2020s.[33] By 2023, interest payments on the debt will exceed the entire defense budget and will be larger than all nondefense discretionary spending by 2025.[34]

The major political parties hold distinct and divergent views of how much the debt matters to the health of the American economy.[35] As revenue shortfall mounts, however, defense and nondefense spending alike will increasingly become the focus of political attention, and we can expect some lawmakers to call for precipitous cuts to both. Defense planners already anticipate an "iron triangle of painful tradeoffs" in the 2020s due to the Budget Control Act, the costs of war in the Middle East, and the impending need for systems modernization—a set of dilemmas that will confront the military even before the mounting debt or ballooning entitlement costs are considered.[36] Political polarization makes it less likely that legislators will find common ground on debt-related issues. Indeed, it may ensure that the parties embrace opposing debt-related philosophies and have little incentive to negotiate toward reform or compromise.

A debt-related, polarization-induced standoff could have far-reaching foreign policy consequences. Deep or persistent crises over the debt ceiling could lead creditors to conclude that U.S. debt is unsustainable, prompting them to sell government bonds en masse and inflict serious harm on the dollar and the U.S. global economic role more broadly.[37] Under such conditions, rivals could seek to fragment the international financial systems, thereby depriving the United States of the benefits it enjoys as the most powerful node in global networks. Two particularly concerning measures would be the coalescence of incipient alternatives to the centralized Society for Worldwide Interbank Financial Telecommunication (SWIFT) global payments system, or a redoubled push by China to displace the dollar through internationalization of its currency, the RMB, including through innovative means like cryptocurrency.[38] Polarization by no means guarantees that a debt crisis will undermine dollar primacy; it does, however, make the possibility more likely.

Polarization and Disinformation

Political, information, and media polarization also create inroads for foreign intervention in American domestic politics. A polarized electorate, information environment, and leadership allow foreign actors to manipulate internal political divisions and general social mistrust to their advantage. Information and media polarization manifest to foreign actors how populations can be mobilized through messaging, and give them venues through which to do so. Misinformation and hyper-partisan content are shared on social media as much as or more than traditional media content.[39] Misinformation and disinformation may go unchallenged because polarized media environments filter out dissenting voices, allowing disinformation to cascade. A hyper-partisan information environment can, in turn, lead partisans to hold inaccurate beliefs about the other political party, fracturing the landscape further. Furthermore, exposure to negative views of the opposing party increases the perceived social distance between the parties, exacerbating affective polarization.[40]

The fragmented media environment makes Western democracies, including the United States, especially vulnerable to disinformation campaigns by adversarial governments.[41] Enabled by the internet and social media, these varied kinds of polarization form seams in the American social fabric. Misinformation campaigns by adversaries are hardly novel, but technology makes them easier and cheaper than ever before. Intense party polarization, moreover, makes it less likely that foreign actors will be punished for disinformation and democratic disruption, as the party that benefits from democratic interference is less apt to support punitive action. Mass polarization has proliferated opportunities for disinformation and disruption, while lowering the price tag of these actions.[42]

Domestic Forces, International Impact

Despite the strong post-2016 inclination to connect major domestic developments with foreign policy outcomes, this is true of only a relatively limited set of domestic trends. This is not to say that no other domestic trends will have a lasting impact on the future of American foreign policy—it is merely to suggest that analysts must demonstrate how precisely a domestic development will act on foreign policy in an enduring manner before they assert that it does, in fact, upend strategy. The hurdles to the U.S. government in harnessing national technological capacity for political ends, and potential disruptions introduced by polarization—as both a primary and an intervening variable—unleash domestic forces that may meaningfully transform the United States' role in the world, and thereby shape international politics itself.

We have identified four issues that political polarization may clearly serve to amplify because of its far-reaching ability to render traditional forms of domestic and international governance unsustainable, but this list is potentially infinite. Moreover, the government–tech sector incentives gap and political polarization may exacerbate one another, with polarization resulting in a turbulent regulatory environment that makes it more difficult still to capture national technological potential. If Washington fails to harness its innovative capacity and does not protect foreign policy from polarization, the results are foreseeably grievous. It will underproduce technologies for national security purposes, underperform its ability to adopt commercial technologies, and have a lumbering government bereft of technological expertise despite its extraordinary resources. Meanwhile, its foreign policy may seem simultaneously deadlocked and erratic, making the country an unpredictable actor in the view of allies and adversaries alike. In such a scenario, even a powerful United States may be substantially hampered in its ability to advance its own interests on the global stage—as a matter both of will and of capability—and thus competitors might increasingly further adverse aims. To understand the true impact of these trends on foreign policy, however, we must consider them alongside the major international forces that are concomitantly shifting America's global role.

THREE

Power, Technology, and a World in Flux

The world the United States faces and its role therein will be shaped as much by international forces as domestic ones. Alongside domestic upheaval, the international system is experiencing epochal geopolitical shifts. The "unipolar moment" in which the United States stood tall as an unrivaled global superpower has waned.[1] The power balance to come will be more complex, but will still confer considerable advantages upon the United States. America will remain the leading economic and military power: its gross domestic product will remain among the world's largest, it will retain unrivaled centrality in the international financial system due to durable dollar dominance, and it will continue to command unique capabilities to project military power around the globe. Yet despite this enduring edge over other nations, the United States' margin of advantage will diminish.

This relative decline will be most acute in Asia, where China's economic growth is fueling its bid for regional hegemony. American allies will have lagging economies and a dwindling share of global military and gross economic power, but the United States will continue to benefit from their economic and technological prowess. Yet global power shifts will also open avenues for new partnerships, as India's formidable military and economic heft as well as rapid growth in several Southeast Asian nations creates an economically multipolar Asia. In this environment, great-power competition will depart from some of its familiar historical features.

Technological change will drive and even accelerate global power shifts, as the domain becomes a central theater of rivalry. Open and closed societies will innovate and adopt technology in fundamentally different ways due to their radically distinct state-society relations—a contrast that is evident in China's use of "digital authoritarianism," particularly when compared to the Washington–Silicon Valley incentives gap. The use of artificial intelligence (AI) for surveillance is just one example of these radically different approaches. Emerging technologies enable new models of domestic, regional, and international order, with rewards conferred upon those who best exploit novel tools for political and material gain, and ultimately set the terms of twenty-first-century governance.

Considered alongside political polarization and the government–tech sector incentives gaps, these international trends have far-reaching implications. They suggest that the United States faces a geopolitical competition with China set in an increasingly multipolar world: a structural condition that is markedly different from its Cold War dynamic with the Soviet Union. This global configuration may be beneficial to the United States if it can marshal its allies toward a common strategy—but it also suggests the potency of middle powers, such as European and Asian allies, or traditionally nonaligned powers like India and Vietnam, which will help to determine balances of power with their alignments. These conditions, moreover, imply the persistence of sub-conventional competition and the difficulty of forming new binding international agreements. If Washington fails to account for these consequential dynamics, it will find itself disadvantaged in increasingly intense forms of modern competition, contending with closed informational and technological zones, and scrambling to protect the norms and rules by which it functions.

Global Power Shifts

Power is the means by which states influence each other in international politics. Although power sometimes takes "softer" forms— such as the attractive force of American popular culture—its "harder" economic and military manifestations are most salient for geopolitics.[2] In particular, economic power allows states to convert their wealth into various instruments of influence, whether financial inducements that entice the cooperation of other states or military capabilities that coerce through the threat or enactment of violence. Precisely because states can fungibly translate economic power into different forms of influence, aggregate national wealth— measured by a state's gross domestic product—is the best single indicator of its actual and potential power. Even so, geopolitical influence is multidimensional and a holistic assessment of global power balances must also account for the per capita distribution of national wealth, the manner in which wealth converts into military capabilities, and the underlying quality of a nation's economy, including its ability to fund technological innovation. While challenging to measure, a state's position in globalized financial, commercial, and technological networks also implicates its ability to exert power—and resist coercion—in an interdependent world.[3]

Three significant forms of global power shifts will therefore shape the world the United States faces over the next fifteen years. China's rise and Russia's revanchism will beget great-power competition. America's NATO and Asia-Pacific allies will confront stagnant growth rates while maintaining economic and technological influence sustained by their formidable market size, human capital endowments, and highly advanced economies. And while China's ascendance casts a long shadow over Asia, the region will be economically multipolar. Together, these power shifts combine to create a novel geostrategic picture for the United States and the world.

China's Rise and Russia's Revanchism

China poses by far the greatest challenge to the United States' preponderant position, emerging as the dominant power in Asia over the coming decade and America's only prospective peer competitor. The United States long benefited from Chinese leaders' fixation on economic growth and internal stability, but since President Xi Jinping assumed office in 2012, Beijing has explicitly sought to re-establish its regional hegemony in Asia.[4] Even if annual growth dips below 5 percent, China is nevertheless on track to be the world's largest economy by 2030 in terms of GDP, and China's technology sector already approaches that of the United States in both R&D spending and market size.[5]

China's growth trajectory, however, is far from assured. Demographically, Beijing's long-standing adherence to the one-child policy will produce a persistently declining population by 2030; as its old-age dependency ratio rises, its public health expenditures will consume larger proportions of the national budget and China's labor force will shrink, with potentially adverse effects on military recruitment.[6] High levels of corporate debt may blunt growth by pushing up interest rates, rationing credit, and potentially provoking financial instability. China's gross GDP estimates may considerably overstate its actual stock of economic and military capabilities, as its national wealth must provide security and services to a vast and geographically diffuse population.[7] Moreover, a perennial question continues to loom large: will China undertake the reform and liberalization necessary to transition to a consumption and service economy? If the answer is yes, Beijing may appear to stumble in the interim but could end up an even more formidable competitor once the transition is complete.

Barring the unlikely prospect of a full economic meltdown, China will continue apace with its military modernization—a structural and technological transformation that has already altered the military balance in East Asia. For the last twenty-five years, China's military budget has grown with its GDP for a 900 percent increase. Beijing's systematic and widespread development of technologically sophisticated capabilities designed to restrict other militaries' operations in the western Pacific—a strategy known as anti-access and area denial, or A2/AD —has already called into question the ability of the United States to mount a direct defense of its Asian allies.[8] Beijing's recent Five-Year Program addresses weaknesses in command structures and force coordination, likely strengthening overall military effectiveness, although some deficiencies remain. Nonetheless, China is already a leading military power in Asia and can rival the United States in the quantitative local balance of military power, as well as advance its influence through political, economic, and military measures short of war, even if it cannot yet extend its might outside of Asia.[9]

Russia, by contrast, will see slow to moderate growth over the next ten to fifteen years but will nonetheless retain the ability to act as a regional and global spoiler.[10] Far from presenting a symmetric challenge, Russia nevertheless maintains areas of considerable military strength and a willingness to tolerate international censure. Moscow will likely experience mediocre growth over the next two decades; without significant economic reforms, the Russian economy will remain highly correlated with hydrocarbon prices and grow modestly at best. It is nonetheless likely to remain the world's sixth-largest economy through 2050, with ample resources to fund its own military modernization.[11]

Russia's recent military interventions, sub-conventional incursions, and nuclear posture foreshadow its future tactics. Moscow's conflicts in Syria and Ukraine, coupled with its continued investments in hybrid, cyber, and nuclear assets, are likely to produce significant integrated unconventional warfare capabilities.[12] These, in turn, will allow it to continue to disrupt the democratic processes of EU and NATO members and pose a real conventional threat to former Soviet states. Russia is unlikely, however, to be able to sustain major military operations against peer competitors beyond its near abroad.[13]

With China's military rise, the United States has lost military primacy in Asia. It will face diminished freedom of action as it contends with growing Chinese military capabilities and regional economic and political power, as well as consequential asymmetric Russian capabilities in Europe. Amid these global power shifts, however, the United States will remain globally mighty. Respectable GDP growth, high levels of immigration, and low borrowing costs drive a stronger growth outlook than its developed peers will enjoy, and the United States will remain the world's largest economy until the late 2020s.[14] The United States retains considerable comparative advantages in technological innovation and, if it can maintain high levels of productivity and efficiency, the country's aggregate wealth may translate into economic and military levers of influence with potency well beyond that implied by global GDP rankings.[15]

Most consequentially, the United States occupies a privileged position in the global financial system with few plausible challenges. Since the conclusion of the Bretton Woods agreement in 1944, the U.S. dollar has served as the global reserve currency. In the absence of a monolithic sovereign debt issuer, the EU is not viewed as a single entity by global competitors or investors, and the euro remains a "currency without a state." China has taken some steps to internationalize the currency, but its markets are still too closed to allow it to sustain a reserve currency role.[16] Moreover, the world continues to rely on the SWIFT system, the network of global financial institutions, which gives the United States commanding influence over global transactions. This "exorbitant privilege" redounds to the

United States' advantage by enabling inexpensive borrowing, entrenching the centrality in financial networks necessary for coercive economic tools like sanctions, and conferring global prestige. Its ability to "weaponize" the interdependence engendered by decades of globalization is enduring and beneficial—particularly as great-power competition assumes an economic character and narrowing margins of military advantage render force a less usable tool of American statecraft.[17]

Despite the loss of military primacy, the United States will remain unrivaled in its ability to project power globally, but adverse local changes—particularly in Asia—will have far-reaching strategic consequences. The U.S. military budget is likely to remain fairly steady, allowing Washington to maintain its lead in producing and operating most high-end weapons systems and platforms for power projection.[18] Nonetheless, Chinese missile capabilities threaten to close the waters of the western Pacific to American military operations, and Russian geographic advantages present a formidable time-distance problem in the Baltics. These circumstances will produce sustained challenges to U.S. strategy, particularly the United States' ability to defend its allies in Asia and Europe. But while the United States will be more constrained in its ability to intervene militarily in these critical regions, China and Russia are unlikely to threaten its global military preponderance. The result will be defense preeminence without hegemony, an advantageous position, but one in which Washington is not guaranteed the ability to secure its defense interests.[19]

Alliance Assets

As global power shifts, Washington's long-standing treaty allies will appear to be economically and demographically sluggish, but they will nevertheless remain quite capable, in some ways increasingly so. Low economic growth may be the new normal for most traditional U.S. allies across Europe and Asia, even as their technological prowess enables significant growth and competitiveness in discrete realms. While several EU nations—as well as the EU bloc more generally—will remain among the world's largest economies, aggregate GDP growth will be lackluster and demographics will drag.[20] European partners nonetheless possess highly educated populations and a fast-growing tech sector, making high-technology growth a likely bright spot, so long as capital, innovation, and entrepreneurship do not flee to other locales.[21]

American allies in Asia also boast economies that are large in scale but slowing in growth, alongside varying levels of military as well as technological capability. South Korea and Australia will experience slow to moderate economic and population growth, whereas Japan's dire demographics contribute to projections of sub-1 percent expansion through 2030. For Asian allies, the technological and military power picture is mixed. Japanese tech firms are in decline, while tech giants in South Korea, especially LG and Samsung, have increased their global prominence and competitiveness.[22] For all of their civilian technological prowess, however, Asian treaty allies face declining military capabilities in comparison to China.[23]

Slow growth and population stagnation have already begun to contribute to constrained allied military spending. Particularly since the end of the Cold War, treaty allies from western Europe to the western Pacific have reduced defense budgets and struggle to meet modest spending targets.[24] Their spending may increase slightly in response to threats from Russia and China, but they will likely continue to underspend relative to their gross economic capacity. The United States can, however, work with its partners to encourage them to spend in ways that are more effective militarily.[25] Even in stagnation, they will remain highly capable, given their large and advanced economies, large per capita incomes, and sophisticated technology bases—although allies in Asia, such as Japan, will likely remain dependent on the United States for their high-end defense as the power balance shifts. Measured against their post–Cold War peak, the United States and its allies have already experienced relative decline across all metrics, and this trend will continue in Asia. Yet their combined economic and technological power will remain formidable over the next decade and beyond, and their prowess in these domains will only gain in geopolitical importance.

Economic Multipolarity in Asia

Even as the United States' traditional allies in Asia idle economically and demographically, however, the broader region will be a major engine of global growth. The Indo-Pacific is likely to develop a lopsided economic multipolarity, whereby China is the largest economy but potentially rivaled in size by India and overtaken in growth rates, though not market size, by Southeast Asian nations. Although Beijing will surely be a heavyweight, India and Southeast Asia provide alternatives to China as sources of regional investment, destinations for foreign money, and links in the global supply chain.

By 2050, four of the world's top ten economies in terms of output will be in Asia (China, India, Indonesia, and Japan) along with two of the three fastest-growing (Philippines and Vietnam). India is by far the biggest and most consequential among this group, as it will be the third-largest economy by 2030.[26] A young, growing population with a long life expectancy will fuel a prolonged economic expansion, even as GDP per capita remains low. Militarily, India now registers the fifth-highest defense budget globally and seeks regional capabilities to project power over land borders and across the Indian Ocean. Its defense industry continues to struggle with project failure and pervasive corruption, however, making it likely to remain a very distant military second to China.[27]

Several Southeast Asian nations—Vietnam, Indonesia, and the Philippines—enjoy strong growth prospects, potentially serving as modest offsets to China's economic heft. Vietnam's anticipated average growth rate of 5 percent or more through 2050 is among the highest in the world. Favorable demographics, as well as an export-oriented economic model with significant foreign direct investment and strategic placement in the global supply chain, bode well for Vietnam's continued success.[28] To its south, Indonesia is projected to become the world's fifth-largest economy by 2030. With vanishingly small R&D investments, Indonesia's large youth population will enable it to compete for jobs at the lower end of the global supply chain. Finally, the Philippines has the fastest growth rate in Southeast Asia. A young population and high fertility rate will likely sustain strong performance in business process outsourcing and technology-enabled services. Despite the fact that all three countries have maritime disputes with China, however, none has overhauled its military in a manner that suggests preparation for regional competition.[29]

China will therefore be regionally preeminent, albeit with some limits. As the next-largest economic and military power with a long-standing rivalry with Beijing, India has the potential to serve as an episodic counterbalance and draw Chinese attention and resources, although it is unlikely to compete with China for regional hegemony. As sizable economies in their own right, smaller Southeast Asian nations will have alternatives to purely bandwagoning with Beijing, although their underdeveloped defense capabilities will still leave them vulnerable to military coercion. Moreover, American allies in the region—Japan, South Korea, and Australia—will retain significant military and economic power that can be maximized if their resources are increasingly networked, both in and outside of the traditional military domain.

These three power shifts combine to create a more vivid picture of twenty-first-century geopolitics: one characterized by a material rivalry between the United States and China within a geopolitically bipolar Asia, nested in a world that is increasingly economically and technologically multipolar. Quite unlike the Cold War, in which lesser powers were sorted into competing blocs, these dynamics suggest that middle powers are likely to retain more flexibility, and with it considerable political and economic influence, despite obvious American and Chinese might. If the United States is able to marshal the strength of its allies toward shared strategic objectives for order in both Europe and Asia, its geopolitical influence will remain commanding. Yet the strength of middle powers alongside China's own ascent suggests that the United States has lost the ability to dictate global governance outcomes alone.

The Future of Technology Governance: Open or Closed?

Traditional measures of power will exert declining influence over geopolitics, as technological innovation and exploitation become a theater of great-power competition. The rate, scope, and nature of technological progress will increasingly reflect fundamental differences between open and closed societies in their public-private relationships. "Techno-authoritarian" models of governance may bestow newfound advantages and vulnerabilities on illiberal regimes, underscoring the urgency of conceiving of technological innovation and adoption as a national security issue—and one that is likely to determine the future of international order itself.

Compared to the disjointed relationship between Washington and Silicon Valley, authoritarian countries have some well-known innovation advantages. Their state-society relations are organized into top-down hierarchies, permitting political leadership to develop and execute national technology strategies with little resistance. They have few boundaries between the private sector and the government, allowing the state to set long-term development goals, target funding, and nurture national champion firms to support its objectives. The lines between the civilian and military domains are permeable, allowing the state to direct and adopt innovation in full support of defense needs and objectives.[30] Since their polities have little expectation of true privacy or free speech, authoritarians can gather and access massive pools of citizen data that democracies simply cannot compile.[31]

China is at the forefront of this movement and developing new means to use technology, personal data, and AI to engineer a more compliant population—notably with its closed internet system, use of widespread surveillance, and export of techno-authoritarianism.[32] Other countries, including Gulf monarchies and Egypt, are following this example, employing AI for policing, censorship, and surveillance; Venezuela recently adopted a new "fatherland" identification card that monitors citizens' social, political, and economic behavior using Chinese technology. While China is pioneering restricted information environments and repressive technological applications at home, it will not simply be able to spread its domestic model of control through the export of these systems to like-minded countries. China's own closed internet relies on a massive party-controlled apparatus and cannot be ready-packaged for other authoritarian regimes.[33] But even short of replication, the diffusion of social-control technologies and the power of China's example will propagate myriad nationally tailored models of tech-enabled governance and, sometimes, repression.

Within states and among them, newer technologies may have transformative political effects: digital surveillance and censorship may solidify regime stability in otherwise vulnerable authoritarian regimes, and applications of AI may provide authoritarian competitors with military advantages that the United States could not obtain as a democratic society. The spread of techno-authoritarianism may also strengthen the coalition of illiberal states that do not share the United States' and its allies' views of internet governance. China has routinely provided digital surveillance training to the governments that receive its exports, and also uses these exchanges as means for garnering support for its preferred "cyber sovereignty" norms.[34] These norms already have the backing of the

Shanghai Cooperation Organization—including Russia—as well as several smaller states friendly to Beijing, and represent the most likely challenge to a free and open internet.

Such techno-normative blocs will shape the future of internet governance—a critical new frontier of international order—and could result in a "splinternet." By spreading aspects of its own closed information system internationally, therefore, Beijing could also export a shuttered form of internet and informational governance that is heavily reliant on AI. A balkanized technological order will be one in which networks are closed off from one another and subject to nation-state regulations with widely variant approaches to privacy, data localization, censorship, and technical standard setting. State-society relations may also shape the extent to which different types of regimes rely on AI-enabled military platforms.[35] For example, in political systems that place less trust in lower-level officers, or in which demographics lead to casualty aversion, AI-enabled unmanned systems may promote escalation by lowering the human and material costs of conflict, offsetting demographic and recruitment problems and mitigating concerns about devolution of authority.[36]

These technological advantages should not invite envy of authoritarian regimes, however. Excessive dependence on data may become a vulnerability if it is corrupted, and state-directed policies can easily lead to suboptimal innovation outcomes. The U.S. model of innovation enjoys advantages of its own, moreover, including a market system that selects for ideas that are more likely to be transformative, and a globally preeminent research university system that acts as an engine of enterprise.[37] These domestic differences will not, however, remain confined to the state level. Democracies' and autocracies' fundamentally different modes of exploiting and spreading technologies are already transforming their visions for international order. The technological domain stands at the nexus of economy and security, but it is all too often sequestered from geopolitical calculations. If American strategy fails to account for the radical differences in technological exploitation in open and closed societies, the country is likely to find itself in a world of ever more restricted information flows without sufficient preparation for the ensuing political and economic consequences.

From Trends to Constraints

Combined with powerful domestic forces, these international drivers will have transformative effects on American foreign policy that extend far beyond the shock of the Trump presidency and will prevent the simple restoration of the country to its traditional post-Cold War role under a new chief executive. First, for U.S. strategists, the most significant geopolitical shift is the demise of American military primacy—a denouement that has already occurred. The country will remain economically, politically, technologically, and militarily mighty, but the condition of near-parity in the local military balance in Asia has stripped Washington of the unbridled advantage it has enjoyed since the end of the Cold War. It is no longer guaranteed to secure its military or political objectives in Asia, and while the United States will remain globally formidable, its forces may be stretched thin as they adjust to demands in the western Pacific. As allies and economic multipolarity make Asia a complex strategic theater, American strategy must prioritize this region and adapt to the uncomfortable new reality of constrained freedom of action. Nevertheless, the United States will remain tremendously powerful globally: Washington will retain financial primacy and a level of military and economic power enjoyed by few nations in history, bequeathing it significant abilities to shape outcomes through national strategy and approaches to governance. The geopolitical environment of the next ten to fifteen years will be a significantly more competitive one than Washington has confronted in three decades, with contours that are unfamiliar, yet still quite favorable.

Second, power shifts have heralded a return to great-power competition with Russia and China, even as these challengers have divergent interests and trajectories. China is a power in unequivocal ascendance, while Russia will remain in abject decline, giving the two some fundamentally divergent medium and long-term interests. Shared borders and self-conceptions as regional leaders portend further friction. Nevertheless, Beijing and Moscow have some shorter-term convergence: both nations are personalist authoritarian regimes that are fearful of aspects of liberalism and seek to dilute U.S. global influence. Geopolitics may therefore assume an ideological tinge, but American strategists should resist Cold War analogies that envision a world cleanly divided by regime type.

Third, this dawning era of geopolitics is likely to be characterized by persistent nonmilitary competition and conflict, often referred to as "gray zone" conflict. Such competition will include activities as diverse as maritime and territorial opportunism using law enforcement or paramilitary forces, disinformation and political warfare campaigns, incursions in cyberspace, and economic coercion. When rivals resort to gray zone tactics, they seek to advance their strategic aims while avoiding existing deterrent thresholds, thereby averting outright war. China and Russia have distinct incentives that lead them to prefer sub-conventional competition: Russia has waning material means, and while China is increasingly potent, its desire to keep rising makes it somewhat risk averse. Both Russia and China possess the ability to engage in devastating interstate conflict with the United States, but each would prefer to reduce risk and preserve resources, leading them to pursue disruptive strategies through subtler approaches. For China, which has the power to spread its own preferences for information governance and order, the technological domain will remain an obvious vector. Nonmilitary competition, particularly in the technological and economic domains, is therefore likely to be a defining feature of geopolitics, and not an ephemeral or self-limiting irritation.

Fourth, although the United States and China are likely to be persistent competitors in Asia, the rise of other economies and the endurance of capable U.S. allies will make regional dynamics far more complex than a strictly bipolar Cold War analogy would suggest. With competition occurring largely in nonmilitary domains, middle powers—both allied and not—will hold significant economic, technological, and political power. The world is unlikely to sort into blocs or camps along neat ideological lines, in part because it is not in the U.S. or Chinese interest to encourage it. With significant growth taking place in mixed-regime economies, both Washington and Beijing will want to partner with up-and-comers where possible, even if they cannot demand full alignment. This geopolitical dynamism heightens the premium on allies that are invested in shared strategy; furthermore, it indicates that case-by-case coalitions will be more diplomatically taxing than either Cold War bipolarity or post–Cold War unipolarity. The United States will be compelled to compete to set the terms for twenty-first-century order, and different areas of order may rely on different coalitions.

Fifth, U.S. domestic dysfunction and international governance paralysis mean that formal interstate cooperation faces newfound challenges; in emerging domains of conflict and cooperation, new legal regimes are unlikely. The United States is passing ever fewer formal international agreements, with a precipitous decline in treaty ratifications, and the international community is similarly stalled in its progress on multilateral accords. Political polarization is likely to blame on the domestic level; internationally, increased competition makes it difficult to identify interest convergence and to insulate cooperation from rivalry. Moreover, the sheer complexity of issues that remain un- or undergoverned requires agreement among a wider and more diverse array of stakeholders. These trends make improbable the coalescence of new regimes to govern emerging domains of conflict and cooperation. The UN is highly unlikely to adopt new international law related to all forms of nonmilitary competition, for example, and democracies and autocracies will probably find it impossible to reconcile their views of tech governance, ensconced as they are in state-society models. A new American approach must seek to set new thresholds and norms, such as those defining and governing conflict in cyberspace, despite the fact that formal rules and institutions—especially those with universal adherence—are far harder to construct than they have been in the past.

Many of the constraints to which American strategy must respond are internal: these include the imperatives to bolster national power, overcome partisan polarization, and reach a productive accommodation between the federal government and the tech sector. Yet the power shifts analyzed here mean that the United States has lost the ability to set the terms of order unilaterally, particularly in Asia. Without primacy, Washington will manage to build new forms of order in the most urgent and contentious of spaces only if it does so with its allies in Europe and Asia, and with other middle powers that share its objectives. Indeed, the convergence of major powers' preferences will be the fulcrums upon which the future of global order will rest, and those preferences themselves are the subject of heated contest.

FOUR

The Contest for
Twenty-First-Century Order

The liberal international order will not survive the tectonic movements under way. International order is dynamic: it changes with global power, as patterns of strategic interaction among states transform. As the United States considers how to renovate the existing order and create new forms of global governance in emerging domains, it cannot proceed unilaterally. Any strategy must account for the preferences and priorities of other major actors whose objectives will become more prominent as power shifts: most crucially China, Russia, India, Japan, and Germany. While far from exhaustive, this set of states best represents the geopolitical landscape Washington will confront. Shifting balances of military, economic, and technological power mean the United States will be unable to secure its preferred forms of order alone.

Unsurprisingly, the greatest challenge to the United States' preferred forms of order emanates from illiberal great powers, primarily China and secondarily Russia, that seek regional spheres of influence. Although the United States must work with Beijing and Moscow in institutions in which they are already leading members,

Washington should resist both states' efforts to remold global and regional order along more authoritarian-friendly lines through institutional entrepreneurship or outright spoiling. If these rival efforts succeed, they may have the effect of shuttering pieces of the international system. This development would be strictly inimical to American security and economic interests, which have long relied on international order to provide access, interdependence, and exchange.

As America propagates its own order vision, India will be a critical hinge state: its potential normative alignment with the United States may make it a partner in building new governance structures and resisting malign revisionism—yet this alignment is far from guaranteed, and a future order must accommodate Delhi's demands for enhanced status, codified in institutional representation in venues like the UN. Long-standing allies like Germany and Japan will be essential force multipliers in competition over the future of international order, with values and capabilities able to advance shared ordering objectives. As these leading states execute their ordering strategies, patterns of conflict and cooperation will not be uniform—rather, as with most historical instances, twenty-first-century order will entail differentiated regional, global, and functional layers, each reflecting distinct convergences of power and interests.

In the contest for order, competition over the future of Asia and global technology governance will be most acute, while existing economic and security regimes require cooperative renovation if they are to survive in their current universal forms. The WTO includes all of the world's most powerful states, but divergent trade preferences may preclude necessary modernization and terminally fell that institution. Global security regimes are essentially stable, with the UN's deference toward great powers satisfying the preferences of most major players, although some revisions to the UN Security Council may be necessary. At the regional level, the future of the Asian order will be hotly contested: China intends to shape regional order through institutional, legal, and normative entrepreneurship—yet Japan and, in some instances, India can stand together with the United States as bulwarks against those forms of Chinese revisionism, like sub-conventional attempts to upend the Asian security order, that may precede a closed sphere of influence. In Europe, Russia lacks the power base or regional allies required for effective order building; to resist its revanchist disruptions, NATO and EU members like Germany will remain ballasts of openness. In all, the United States and its allies can secure a favorable and accessible future order, despite the dusk of the liberal international order. Guaranteeing an open order despite opposing forces of closure, however, will require a lucid American vision alongside shrewd statecraft.

China

The Chinese Communist Party (CCP) has adopted a mixed strategy toward international order. Although the CCP appears committed to many of the order's rules at the international level, Beijing flouts them regionally, given its power to set norms and advance its interests. As a result, the CCP has, in many cases, acceded to various international regimes without fully implementing or committing to the norms and policies that these institutions espouse. Yet Beijing does not simply contest unfavorable elements of the extant order from within—it is actively constructing new forms of order both globally and regionally through vigorous norm entrepreneurship and energetic institution building, writing new rules where few exist. For all that China's vision of global order is nascent, the outlines of international and regional orders with Chinese characteristics are coming into sharper focus.[1]

A Mixed Global Strategy

Globally, the People's Republic of China (PRC) tends to support the order's rules, laws, and norms. In its institutional membership, it is as participatory as any country besides the United States and a particularly active member of the UN system. As a permanent member of the UN Security Council (UNSC), Beijing has increased its funding to the UN overall and its support of peacekeeping in particular, with budget contributions second only to the United States. Where liberal values seem to directly menace the Chinese regime, the CCP has pursued normative revision from within existing institutions—for example, by acceding to human rights treaties or international human rights bodies and then flouting their core tenets. Despite its well-documented human rights abuses at home, which have only accelerated since Xi Jinping assumed power, the PRC is a founding member of the UN Human Rights Council (UNHRC) and a signatory of more than twenty international human rights conventions and protocols. The PRC's use of this forum illustrates how—without sufficient pushback from the United States and like-minded nations—authoritarian states can co-opt institutions to neuter their norms. The CCP increasingly relies on the UNHRC to bolster its own agenda-setting power, silence criticism of Chinese practices, and diminish accountability for human rights violations. These practices create a global governance climate friendlier to domestic closure.[2]

Beijing's approach to international order reform is similarly nuanced. The CCP seeks greater influence over global bodies like the IMF and G20; by seeking reforms that enhance its own representation, Beijing appears interested in advancing international agendas that align more closely with China's, particularly in the development realm.[3] Where extant economic and security regimes benefit China—whether by design or default—Beijing has proven far more resistant to meaningful reforms. The PRC has all but broken the WTO, due to the prejudicial structure of the Chinese economy, the CCP's unwillingness to reform, and the WTO's ill preparedness to deal with the impasse, rather than specific actions by Beijing to expressly violate existing rules. The WTO was and remains wholly unprepared to deal with China—but, by virtue of its membership and the organization's consensus-based decision making, WTO reform cannot proceed without Chinese assent, and Beijing's interest in facilitating change is limited. China has also resisted attempts to modify UNSC membership, not wanting to dilute its own voting power or introduce new veto players. China's cooperation is therefore needed to renovate legacy international institutions—but, particularly in the WTO and UN, its interests are contrary to those of the United States, making meaningful progress unlikely.

By contrast, China is far more activist in new ordering domains where it identifies opportunities to build favorable global governance structures. As global power shifts confer additional influence on Beijing, the CCP will attempt to shape burgeoning rules in ungoverned areas such as cyberspace, AI, and the internet, alongside a continued inclination to exploit gaps in existing rules and institutions. The PRC's vision for the future of technological governance is explicitly at odds with the priorities of an open international system. China has spearheaded UN efforts to keep internet, AI, and cyberspace rule making as well as technical standards setting within state purview, partly by lobbying for routes that are "multilateral" (signifying rule making by states) rather than "multi-stakeholder" (involving consultations with nongovernmental actors, including civil society, businesses, and academic institutions). Accordingly, the CCP's broader vision for multilateral internet governance would permit discrete national cyber spheres populated with state-approved content—an approach that is backed by Russia and other states with authoritarian or mixed regimes.[4]

Even as some domains of future order will be vigorously contested, climate remains a potentially fruitful—and existentially necessary—area of cooperation. On climate change, the PRC now stands as the global leader, albeit through self-interest and by default. The PRC faces massive environmental fallout from its remarkable pattern of growth over the last four decades, with real consequences for public health in terms of air quality, life expectancy, and water contamination and scarcity. Recognizing this fact, the PRC appears poised to meet its commitments under the Paris Agreement and has taken steps to rebalance its energy mix, shifting away from coal and toward renewables such as wind and solar. Yet it remains the planet's largest carbon dioxide emitter and has backed at least one hundred new coal-fired power plants as part of its Belt and Road Initiative (BRI), indicating only partial compliance with the emerging international climate regime. The PRC's increasing contributions should not mask the selective nature of its leadership on climate issues.[5]

China's Regional Revisionism

Within Asia, the PRC has sought changes to or directly challenged existing forms of order—steps that may create an environment far friendlier to closed forms of domestic and international governance. Beijing's revisionism is most focused on regional security issues. From its heterodox interpretation of the UN Convention on the Law of the Sea (UNCLOS) and South China Sea island-building campaign to its leaky valve status on North Korea sanctions enforcement to its proven ability to deadlock and scuttle Association of Southeast Asian Nations measures, Beijing has often secured its interests by selectively challenging rules without replacing them. It remains frustrated with and opposed to U.S. alliances as relics of the Cold War; in its effort to undermine their legitimacy, Beijing has advanced a "community of common destiny," which seeks to replace U.S. alliances and make order friendlier to nondemocracies. Previous efforts to supplant America's alliances with new Chinese concepts have failed, but the CCP's long-held grievances with the current architecture still abound. Nevertheless, the PRC has been able to advance its South China Sea claims without activating American alliance commitments or provoking direct conflict. In most of these cases, the PRC has not expressly sought scofflaw status; often, it actually uses existing rules to hinder prevailing institutions when they are prejudicial to its security interests, employing an arbitration exception clause to UNCLOS or exploiting ASEAN's reliance on consensus. In advancing its island claims as long-standing matters of sovereignty, it is actually invoking rules-based aspects of order, however disingenuously.[6]

Beyond these efforts to chip away at the extant security order, Beijing is also building an institutional superstructure that may support Chinese regional hegemony. Having experimented with security and economic cooperation through the Shanghai Cooperation Organization (SCO), Beijing has increasingly turned toward bilateral cooperation unconstrained by multilateral decision-making constraints and, in the SCO's case, consensus norms. The Asian Infrastructure Investment Bank (AIIB) is an important example of Beijing's attempts to revise the regional economic order via institutional entrepreneurship. Despite early angst, including active lobbying against the organization by the Obama administration, it now seems that AIIB will operate with a governance model that is basically consistent with prevailing international standards—at least in part because it brought in retired World Bank experts to draft its charter and design its environmental and social framework. Thus far, the AIIB has lent relatively little of its own money (about $4.4 billion) and been highly cooperative with other development banks via major co-financing arrangements. Though AIIB's character may change over time, early concerns about its aims have not been borne out.[7]

The future of BRI is far less certain, but its ambition to blanket the Eurasian continent as well as space and cyberspace raises the possibility that it could become a vector of Chinese dominance. BRI—which may result in over $1 trillion in Chinese outlays within the decade—includes several different types of projects, such as traditional and digital infrastructure projects awarded to Chinese state-owned enterprises (SOEs), economic development projects that may bring substantial benefits to recipient states, and facilities that may even have military implications. Yet BRI remains elusively undefined, and there are no criteria for what constitutes a BRI project, nor any reliable accounting of its true scope. The initiative is undeniably answering regional infrastructure needs, but in select cases may load host countries with unsustainable debt, particularly if they are already vulnerable by virtue of poor state capacity. Malaysia, Myanmar, Nepal, and Sri Lanka have either been unable to repay Chinese loans or suspended BRI-sponsored projects for fear of ballooning debt burdens. More commonly, projects run aground due to poor administration by the Chinese government and companies. Nonetheless, its reach continues to expand globally, with Italy, an American treaty ally, signing twenty-nine separate deals worth roughly $2.8 billion—signifying BRI's prospective influence in Europe. If BRI's opaque commercial loans routinely proceed with poor administration by Chinese companies, they may exacerbate poor domestic governance in recipient states, giving them few incentives to reform and creating cycles of dependency. Over time, this could lead to an entrenched Chinese model of development that bypasses existing multilateral development banks and systems and spreads considerable Chinese influence. Furthermore, the sprawling nature of BRI means that the CCP may have ample opportunity to create new auxiliary rules and institutions, such as its BRI dispute tribunal system, which is basically an extension of Chinese law. The same vast expanse, however, may expose China to considerable political vulnerabilities that it has not faced before. CCP aspirations notwithstanding, it is simply too soon to tell whether BRI is a viable prototype for Chinese global governance.[8]

China's Rise and the Future of International Order
While China's approach to twenty-first-century order is embryonic, it is clearly the actor most capable of building or changing order in ways that imperil U.S. interests. Beijing alone has the

resources to pioneer like-minded coalitions to change rules and standards to assert its dominance. Such revisionist attempts are most likely to appear in the technological and economic domains—both globally and regionally—and the security order in Asia, while China may remain essentially satisfied with the UN-centric edifice for global political and security cooperation. Any design for future order must aim to co-opt the PRC where possible, as with evolving development norms; seek cooperation where desirable, as on global climate governance; and compete vigorously when necessary, as with the future of technology governance or on existing maritime rules.

Russia

Unlike China, which will have the capacity to build new forms of order in the coming decade, Russia will possess the intent and ability to undermine existing rules and institutions but have far less power to build new ones. From an American perspective, Russia is more a spoiler than a challenger. Much as Moscow would like to rebuild a sphere of influence in its near abroad, its success in doing so has been and will remain quite limited. Instead, its revisionism tends to assume a negative character—rather than offering an alternative vision for regional or international organization, or seeking institutional reforms, Moscow exploits gaps and weaknesses in the existing order in ways that create greater freedom of action for itself. Undermining American influence, whether unilaterally or via alignment with China, is central to this effort. Driven by a desire to actualize its self-image as a great power, Moscow embraces certain institutional features of the post–World War II order, particularly the UN—which elevates Russia as a member of the UNSC—but adheres to its norms only selectively. This approach reflects a skepticism toward rules and norms long evident in Russian strategic culture, which tends to view material power as paramount.[9]

Russia's Global Revisionism

Moscow selectively supports central elements of the postwar international order. As a permanent member of the UNSC, Russia embraces that body, which elevates it alongside the United States as a major power. The UN affords Russia a forum to censure international interferences in others' affairs, as well as to mitigate the international response to Russia's own transgressions, as in Crimea and Ukraine. The UNSC models the type of international order that Russia would like to see—a forum for bargaining among coequal major powers—and Moscow resists reforms that would expand the council's permanent membership. In these efforts, Russia has often found common cause with the PRC: the voting concordance of China and Russia in the UN General Assembly has increased significantly over the post–Cold War period, from 43 percent in 1994 to 78 percent in 2019.[10]

Even as it operates within global security institutions, however, Moscow seeks to undermine the universality of global security norms governing the use of military force. The Russian government vociferously supports these rules when they protect Russia against foreign encroachment or provide standing for critiques of American hypocrisy. But Moscow also brazenly violated foundational nonaggression norms through the 2014 annexation of Crimea and invasion of Ukraine. Similarly, Russia has undermined the human rights regime from within, serving on the UNHRC despite its poor domestic record. Sovereignty is a strategic watchword for Russia, though its leadership seems to believe that only great powers enjoy the right to noninterference—and, as its interference into American elections demonstrates, even that privilege is qualified.[11]

Russia is a relatively new entrant into the WTO-centric free-trade regime, and since its 2012 accession has demonstrated an ambivalent approach to open economic exchange. Although Russia engages procedurally in dispute resolution mechanisms, its compliance with WTO rulings has been mixed, and while Moscow has increased transparency, it largely failed to carry out requisite economic modernization. In particular, Russia continues to enact protectionist policies via nontariff barriers to trade—for example, unduly burdensome import licensing, an opaque customs legal regime, and persistent restrictions on U.S. agricultural exports. Moreover, since the post-2014 imposition of sanctions by the United States and European Union, Russia has doubled down on a policy of import substitution and state control of key industries, most notably energy. While the prejudicial effects of Russian economic policy are limited by its market size and centrality—both of which pale in comparison to China's—they do suggest a trajectory of greater economic closure and even autarky. Russia is increasingly pursuing domestic self-reliance, as well as bilateral trade agreements and oil and gas contracts, in a bid to gain independence from a globalized international economy that exposes it to Western economic coercion.[12]

As order spreads to emerging domains, Russia seeks to maintain its authority by orienting state-based global governance efforts through the UN. Like China, Moscow seeks a multilateral approach to internet governance and data localization that elevates the role of states, rather than private-sector entities or other stakeholders, as the main players. Emphasizing state control over the internet is a means of preventing foreign involvement in its domestic information space. Russia is also trying to shore up its own right to access the information transmitted by citizens within its borders. These efforts reinforce Russia's ascription to the Chinese-backed notion of cyber sovereignty. Russia has also proposed UN pacts that forswear offensive cyber activity, but its own offensive cyber operations belie the seriousness of these governance efforts. Despite its general preference for multilateral instruments, Russia did not sign the only international agreement on cyber crime or the recent Paris Call for Trust and Security in Cyberspace. Russia also opposes the negotiation of international legal agreements on fully autonomous weapons. In addition to internet governance, Russia seeks UN involvement in another increasingly competitive domain: space. Russia has pursued arms control for space weapons via the UN Conference on Disarmament in an apparent attempt to limit the United States' development of missile defense. Together with China, Russia has long advocated a multilateral treaty preventing the placement of weapons in outer space—an effort opposed by Washington.[13]

Regional Revisionism

Within Europe and Central Asia, Russia has demonstrated an interest in building the institutional infrastructure for a sphere of influence, but such efforts have largely fallen short of expectations. The Collective Security Treaty Organization (CSTO), for example, allowed Russia to maintain a residual military presence in Central Asia and facilitates military sales, training, and assistance to CSTO members. Dissatisfaction among member states has hindered the CSTO's efficacy, however, and it is highly unlikely that the CSTO will become an integrated and effective security organization that competes meaningfully with NATO or the EU. In the economic realm, Russia has joined a number of alternative institutions and created some of its own. The Eurasian Economics Union (EAEU), for example, seeks to integrate Russia and post-Soviet states in Central Asia into a new, cohesive economic entity. Yet, as with the CSTO, the EAEU is constrained by its own limitations, as members have demonstrated little interest in economic integration. Moscow may see greater success in alignment with Chinese-led institutions. Russia is the third-largest investor in AIIB, and the EAEU is considering integration with BRI. Since many EAEU members already work with BRI bilaterally, however, the end result may simply be Chinese co-optation.[14]

Otherwise, Russian revisionism has been mostly subtractive in nature: Moscow is increasingly skeptical toward the arms control pillar of the European security order and has curtailed its participation. Russia's leadership fears that bilateral arms control treaties with the United States will restrain Russia's nuclear arsenal while enabling Washington to achieve superiority via ballistic missile defense development. Russia has also withdrawn from the Conventional Forces in Europe Treaty and violated the Intermediate Range Nuclear Forces Treaty, both cornerstones of the Cold War arms control regime. Even so, Moscow continues to see value in strategic arms agreements like the New START Treaty, though its lifespan beyond 2021 remains uncertain.[15]

Russia and the Future of International Order

Ultimately, Russia has little interest in order modernization as it awaits the dusk of American hegemony and dawn of a new, multipolar era. As Russian analyst Dimitri Trenin puts it: "On broader issues of world order, Russia has offered no alternative design to what exists today and no comprehensive reform blueprint."[16] Instead, Russia's goals lie more in negating the elements of the liberal international order that constrain its ability to act freely at home, in its region, and globally. For now, the Russian government sees a closer alignment with China as furthering these aims. A balancing partnership with China allows Russia to work toward a world where it has greater sovereignty and flexibility, while also reaping the benefit of intensified economic exchange and investment in the Far East. Yet there are indications that Moscow recognizes the limitations of its closer ties with China, and their shared commitment to authoritarianism reflects a thin ideological alignment that is unlikely to produce sustained cooperation over time. Russia is clearly the subordinate state in the relationship—a position it hardly relishes— and eventual Chinese regional hegemony could prove quite threatening to Russia, given the nations' shared borders and overlapping notional spheres of influence. This dynamic may ultimately create space for U.S.-Russia cooperation on international or regional governance—but until that time, American strategy should assume its collaboration will be issue-specific, interest-based, and fairly transitory.

India

India will play a decisive role in the contest between models of twenty-first-century order. In many areas, Delhi's interests accord with Washington's: it eschews interstate aggression and elevates peaceful dispute resolution, embraces economic integration, encourages open access to the global commons, and emphasizes sovereignty and territorial integrity. Regionally, India welcomes American security leadership in Asia and shares acute concern about prospective Chinese hegemony. Delhi's strategy for international order implies only mild revisionism: it generally does not seek to overturn existing norms, rules, and institutions either at a global or regional level, but it does demand greater representation. To the extent that American strategy can harness this desire for increased influence over order making, India may serve as an ordering partner. But even so, its alignment will be neither guaranteed nor absolute. Under Prime Minister Narendra Modi, Delhi has become more willing to use force to settle border disputes with Pakistan and to target Muslim minorities at home in a manner inconsistent with liberal human rights norms. Moreover, India's long-standing emphasis on sovereignty leaves room for cooperation with states like China and Russia, which see noninterference as compatible with closure, and Delhi's self-image as a champion of the developing world may motivate demands for differential treatment that undermines reciprocal rule making.[17]

Seeking Global Power and Prestige

India mostly embraces the principles underlying the existing international order, even as Delhi seeks institutional reforms that will give it more power and prestige. Rather than overturning the institutional core of the post–World War II system, India seeks to strengthen it through modernization. Greater inclusion of developing nations is a core demand, and India has long campaigned for a permanent seat on the UNSC. As a nuclear weapons state that sits outside the Nonproliferation Treaty (NPT), Delhi also seeks the privileges conferred on other atomic powers, like inclusion in the Nuclear Suppliers Group (NSG).[18]

Delhi's status-based objections extend to the international economic order: although Delhi views participation in the free trade regime as essential to its growth trajectory, it also believes international financial institutions suffer from systematic biases against developing nations. As a WTO member, Delhi has called for equity-enhancing reforms to both processes and rules; for example, India vigorously objects to the acceptance of European and American agricultural subsidies while India's own Public Distribution System of food to the poor is deemed a market-distorting system. Delhi has also criticized the internal voting architecture of organizations like the World Bank and the IMF, asserting that they favor countries like the United States while giving little voice to developing nations' interests. India therefore regularly calls for the voting quotas of the organizations to be reevaluated. To bolster these calls for reform, India has also engaged in some moderate institutional entrepreneurship, joining with "BRICS" partners Brazil, Russia, China, and South Africa to create the New Development Bank in 2014, an international financial institution capitalized by the consortium of then-promising economies.[19]

The extent to which India's interests align with those of fellow emerging powers like China versus fellow democracies like the United States will have critical bearing on the shape of future order. This conflict is likely to play out most acutely as governance coalesces in new domains. In shaping internet governance, for example, some of India's preferences have overlapped with those of liberal states: under pressure from civil society and business, India has advocated a multi-stakeholder internet (the Western position), defended net neutrality, and its Supreme Court upheld the privacy of citizens' personal data. At the same time, however, India has taken steps that bear more similarity to China and other illiberal states' positions on cyber sovereignty. Prime Minister Modi has proposed regulations that would curtail activity by Western technology companies and potentially infringe upon Indians' privacy and freedom of speech. These prospective changes build on past attempts to regulate freedom of expression online: in 2019, India's national, state, and local governments shut down the internet nearly one hundred times—far more frequently than any other country. Delhi's ultimate alignment will determine the future of internet governance for a massive swath of the global population; if India moves toward a closed information environment, the balance of ideas may tip in China's favor.[20]

Moreover, in some instances, India's vision of order entails special, rather than strictly equal, treatment for developing nations—a perspective China shares. India, like China, remains insistent that the global climate change regime should have a two-track approach that differentiates between developed and developing countries— for example, by establishing separate requirements for the two categories and providing financial aid for the latter. Additionally, despite decades of domestic economic liberalization, there is some indication that development pressures are turning India away from the principles of international economic openness. Both major political parties have considered abandoning economic liberalization because of unemployment and the tensions surrounding simultaneous urbanization and industrialization. If India's current growth model continues to slump, it may embrace a more state-run or universal basic income–driven model of economic growth. Modi has already taken steps that might be consistent with such a shift, although they remain modest and reversible. These examples illustrate India's hinge position—given its unique constellation of interests, Washington will have to compete for Delhi's support and would be misguided to assume alignment on the basis of democratic regime type alone.[21]

Soft Regional Revisionism

Regionally, India supports the vision of a free, open, and inclusive Indo-Pacific where countries are able to make their own choices, free from foreign intervention or pressure. Although Delhi does not object to the United States' presence—and has actually embraced greater bilateral military cooperation in recent years—it envisions a militarily and economically multipolar Indo-Pacific in which India plays a larger role. A multipolar Asia would be institutionally integrated through standing multilateral structures like ASEAN as well as less formal groupings like the Quadrilateral Security Dialogue ("Quad") with the United States, Japan, and Australia. Given its historical commitment to strategic autonomy, India prefers to address regional security issues through these flexible arrangements rather than fixed alliances, so long as its archrival Pakistan is excluded. For India, alignment on matters of regional governance flows from interests, not ideology: in pursuit of an open regional order, Delhi is agnostic about regime type and seeks pragmatic partnerships with authoritarian countries like Singapore, Thailand, and Vietnam to counterbalance a rising China.[22]

Indeed, the greatest threat to India's vision of a multipolar Asian regional order is China—with which India has maritime and territorial tensions—and Delhi seeks to forestall Beijing's dominance. This imperative has motivated a differentiated strategy toward China-led regional economic initiatives: India is a founding member and the second-largest shareholder of AIIB, but it boycotted BRI. Whereas India sees AIIB as complementary to the norms of the international economic order, Delhi has voiced concerns about BRI's lack of transparency and good governance, and is generally wary of the possibility that it will bolster Chinese influence in South Asia.[23]

A "Hinge" State

Over the next ten to fifteen years, India will continue to be an active participant in international order, but its national interests make it something of a "hinge" power between Western liberal democracies and rising illiberal powers. Given its long-standing commitment to strategic autonomy, India is unlikely to align entirely with either the United States or China, instead preferring multipolar power and governance structures that elevate Delhi's voice. On most matters of global as well as regional governance, India is likely to make issue-specific determinations in its support for various forms of order reform or revision. Delhi may therefore seek to counterbalance China's rise through enhanced partnerships with the United States and even Russia at the same time as it makes common cause with China on issues of sovereignty, technological rule making, or trade protectionism.

Japan

In its postwar decision to abjure the use of force and major national military capability, Japan became more invested in international order than virtually any other country. Japan's longtime membership in regional and global economic institutions such as the IMF, WTO, and ASEAN reflects its belief that multilateralism can bring development and stability. In the twenty-first century, Tokyo balances two increasingly tense foreign policy interests—the alliance with the United States and diplomacy with China—by participating in and leveraging the international and Asian regional orders to its benefit. Through its alliance with Washington, Tokyo seeks national security, and through ties with China, economic security. Despite this delicate equilibrium, Japan's liberal democratic values and national interests motivate an unambiguous preference for "free and open" regional as well as international orders that feature American leadership and foreclose Chinese dominance.[24]

Strengthening the Global Status Quo

Since Article 9 of the Japanese constitution rejects the use of force as a tool of statecraft, Tokyo has long emphasized institutions and multilateral action under the UN Charter as its preferred approaches to global problems. Japan is a major financial and personnel contributor to the UN; after years as the second-largest contributor to the UN general budget, it fell into third place behind China in 2019.[25] Tokyo has raised its profile on global human rights issues through the UNHRC, increased its contributions to peacekeeping, and sought more international cooperation on maritime and environmental issues. While Japan has often mirrored the United States' positions in the UN, it has also supported UNSC reform to improve the body's legitimacy, effectiveness, representativeness, and transparency. In these efforts, Japan has coordinated its position with India, Brazil, and Germany. The group advocates for a UNSC with a membership of twenty-five, including six new permanent members (Brazil, Japan, Germany, India, and two African countries) and an additional three elected seats. A supporter of the international economic order, Japan seeks to strengthen it through WTO reform. Tokyo collaborated with the United States and the EU to submit a joint reform proposal related to subsidy violations—a proposal clearly crafted with China in mind. Further, Prime Minister Shinzo Abe made rebuilding trust in the global trade system, including WTO reforms, a central pillar of his G20 chairmanship.[26]

Concerning governance in new technological domains, Tokyo's positions have generally tracked with Washington's. Japan has been consistently supportive of a multi-stakeholder model of internet governance. Tokyo generally promotes free speech and access to information over and above privacy issues, but it passed a 2018 regulation intended to align with the EU's General Data Protection Regulation (GDPR). On cyber governance, Tokyo has taken a position consistent with the Tallinn consensus that existing international law, including the law of armed conflict, applies in cyberspace, and seeks to build new norms for the peacetime uses of cyberspace. Taken together, Tokyo's preliminary moves in new tech domains suggest that is likely to seek forms of internet, cyber, and AI governance that are consistent with those sought by the United States and the EU. It has also sought coordination with like-minded countries in the space domain, with an eye to applying and strengthening the rule of law, and to developing international regulations and confidence-building measures.[27]

Resisting Regional Revisionism

Japan supports new institutions and rules when they help to fill the gap between the United States' diminished relative power and predictability and China's expansive regional aims. For Tokyo, this strategy implies some limited participation in Chinese institutions as well as status quo–oriented entrepreneurship of its own. Like the United States, Japan has opposed China's creation of new institutions, notably AIIB and BRI. With the United States having largely disengaged on these issues since 2016, however, Tokyo has joined BRI in a limited capacity, hoping to shape its implications for order from within. Tokyo may also join the AIIB.[28]

In 2014, Japanese leaders introduced the Free and Open Indo-Pacific Strategy (FOIPS) as a counterweight to Chinese models of regional order. FOIPS envisions an open Asia and includes a Japanese response to BRI. Japan recognizes that it does not have China's economic capacity, but touts the transparency and higher standards of its efforts, distinguishing its approach from China's BRI model. Indeed, Tokyo has long used economic aid as a tool of statecraft but has increased its giving and tied it more clearly to security aims in recent years. In 2015, Japan was the fourth-largest global provider of aid, at around $10 billion annually. This aid is a form of regional competition with China. Tokyo has become increasingly focused on providing military equipment and training to Southeast Asian countries like Vietnam and the Philippines, both of which are counter-claimants to China in the South China Sea. In so doing, Tokyo hopes to bolster these countries' ability to stand against China, where it may undermine the rule of law and the balance of power.[29]

Japan's desire to preserve the order's liberal economic values has led it to assume the role of a regional trade entrepreneur. Even as the United States under Trump has rejected free-trade principles, Japan remains strongly supportive of them and has filled a trade leadership vacuum on the Trans-Pacific Partnership (TPP). American withdrawal from TPP immediately undermined Tokyo's leading rationales for the multilateral pact: to smooth divisive market issues with Washington and to anchor the United States to a trade regime in Asia as China becomes the regional economic powerhouse. Nonetheless, Tokyo helped to lead other middle powers, especially Australia and New Zealand, to adjust and conclude the agreement, now known as the Comprehensive and Progressive Agreement for Trans-Pacific Partnership (CPTPP). Tokyo's efforts to establish new trade and development structures are ultimately designed to preserve the international order's liberal economic norms rather than to redefine them. By establishing alternative, if asymmetric, structures to compensate for the U.S. abdication of economic leadership in the face of China's ascent, Japan's new initiatives have status quo aims.[30]

Similar objectives have motivated novel enterprises in the regional security realm. In 2016, Japan put forward a proposal for an ASEAN-wide defense framework, which is intended to help Japan begin or expand partnerships with countries in Southeast Asia. These regional strategic partnerships, such as those with Australia and the Philippines, include defense and security agreements below the level of full alliances, and are part of U.S. backed efforts to encourage mutually beneficial security ties among like-minded

Asia-Pacific countries. It also continues to deepen bilateral ties with India through economic and security cooperation, and has embraced the U.S.-Japan-Australia-India Quadrilateral Security Dialogue. Japan's quest to strengthen existing rules and norms through new regional frameworks suggests it is contemplating a vision of broader cooperation to support a free and open Indo-Pacific order as it becomes less feasible to rely on a single American guarantor.[31]

An Uncertain Future

Japan is among the most active proponents of openness both globally and within Asia. It seeks to protect itself from adverse shifts in the regional security order due to China's rise, to reinforce the regional economic order as Beijing continues to ascend and Washington stumbles, and to engage a more diverse set of regional and global actors in preserving the liberal character of prevailing norms and rules. While Tokyo cannot uphold an open system by itself, its material endowments, network of partnerships, and strategic entrepreneurship will make it an eager and invaluable ally as the United States resists forces of regional as well as international closure.

Germany

Over the coming decade, Germany will remain the most influential European power and a leader within the EU, with attendant abilities to influence the norms, laws, and institutions that regulate international conflict and cooperation. Germany intends to use that power in a bid to preserve the status quo both regionally and globally. This strategic commitment reflects significant benefits Germany has accrued from its participation in the post–Cold War order: political influence independently and via EU leadership, economic prosperity amid fertile export markets facilitated by the free-trade system, and ample security within NATO and under the American nuclear umbrella. Even as domestic and international realities increasingly belie the optimism of Berlin's strategy, it has not yet reckoned with the challenges to order—whether from a rising China, revanchist Russia, unreliable United States, stagnant EU, or increasingly polarized and populist domestic public. Its approach to international order is thus one of hopeful preservation: Berlin seeks to strengthen the order through minor reforms but envisions no significant overhaul.[32]

Global Steward

Germany is a bulwark of liberalism, deeply committed to democracy, human rights, and multilateral cooperation on a range of global governance challenges, even as it also seeks modest procedural reforms to postwar institutions. The fourth-largest UN contributor, Berlin advocates for modifications to the UNSC that would enhance Berlin's influence, joining Japan, Brazil, and India in a collective call for reform. On matters of international economic governance, Germany is aligned with an open trading regime and supports institutional modernizations that advance such aims. Berlin backs reforms to the WTO—specifically, expanded representation of countries; stronger monitoring of members' trade policies, particularly related to state subsidies; and more effective mechanisms of dispute settlement, including changes to the Appellate Body.[33]

As a powerful force within the EU, Germany is guiding Europe's approach to new global governance regimes. A long-standing leader on climate change and signatory to the Paris Agreement, Germany has introduced an implementation initiative to help developing countries comply by giving financial assistance. Berlin has also taken a leadership role in technology governance: it clearly sees Europe as a maker rather than taker of internet governance and recognizes the importance of collective action. Within the EU, a wave of regulation—most notably the GDPR—has pioneered new standards for issues like privacy, data localization, and algorithmic decisions. Applying to any company operating in the EU, the GDPR has significant extra-territorial reach, and its implementation immediately reshaped the global tech landscape. Whether the EU is able to parlay its regulation into a globalized framework for technological governance will depend on two factors: first, whether the European emphasis on privacy and regulation is compatible with an open information ecosystem, and second, the extent to which Europe can coordinate like-minded partners, including the United States, to advance consistent standards. If either falls short, there is a risk of a distinctly European internet that splinters both from an open American-led internet and a Chinese internet that privileges state surveillance and control.[34]

Regional Stalwart

Germany is unequivocally committed to a Europe more tightly integrated through economic and defense cooperation. Berlin advocates financial integration, including a capital market union, and has pushed to expand the digital single market within Europe. Germany is also growing increasingly supportive of security and defense cooperation under EU auspices, including on defense research funding and military integration. Such small-scale European defense integration could eventually replace the need for U.S. forces in small to medium crisis management operations—though Berlin insists these arrangements are strictly complementary to NATO. Indeed, NATO remains a cornerstone of Berlin's foreign policy: As one of the alliance's largest contributors in absolute terms, Germany has increased its defense spending, though it stands at just 1.22 percent of Germany's GDP, with plans to reach 1.5 percent by 2024, and Berlin also makes active, if moderate, contributions to combat missions in Afghanistan and Kosovo.[35]

These multilateral frameworks structure Germany's approach to potential threats to the European regional order—namely, Russian aggression and subversion as well as growing Chinese economic encroachment. Germany sees Russia as a traditional security threat, given shared historical legacies, geographic proximity, and Putin's preference for disruption of European order. For Germany's strategic elite, China has only recently emerged as a challenge, given that Berlin has few immediate security concerns in Asia. Beijing is, however, increasingly seen as a peer competitor in the global economy, and a potential challenger to Germany's conception of European order. Whereas Germany seeks to act via NATO in addressing Russia's military threat, it prefers to coordinate an EU response to China without the United States, particularly given Washington's go-it-alone China policy.

Future Disruption?

Germany's strategy for order faces international and domestic pressures. Domestically, right-wing political forces unhappy with German policies—especially on immigration—challenge liberal values as well the country's foundational commitment to ever-closer European integration via the EU. Similar trends call into question the future of German trade liberalization. Germany's global influence is also densely intertwined with the EU's prospects, as EU leadership amplifies Berlin's global sway even as it also mediates German preferences via intrabloc bargaining. Sociopolitical upheaval throughout Europe menaces the overall integrity of the European Union—from Brexit and persistent weaknesses in the southern eurozone economies to illiberal backsliding in Hungary and Poland—and casts doubt on its ability to present a unified front on all dimensions of future order. Absent a precipitous disintegration, the EU will remain a central player in shaping the European security, economic, technological, and political order. In those areas where it can muster the requisite cohesion, the EU has the economic and technological heft to pioneer or shape future forms of global order, as with its foray into internet governance with GDPR, or multilateral trade agreements like a prospective Euro-Pacific trade deal. With a diminished, divided, or normatively reoriented EU, however, the bloc's—and, by extension, Germany's—influence over international governance and its negotiating leverage within the free-trade system would flag. If Europe can continue to stave off these forces, Berlin will stand as a leader of a bloc integral to the future of an open international system—and one that will align significantly, if not entirely, with the United States' ordering preferences.[36]

Into the Breach

With numerous global actors all pursuing their own grand strategy and vision for the future of international order as global power shifts, the status quo is under significant strain. While the liberal international order was never a monolithic set of structures with a coherent agenda, it represented an aspirational set of principles whose universalist claims have already become fiercely contested by illiberal challengers. Revisionists of various stripes are largely embedded in existing forms of order, seeking to erode it both from within and without. Where victorious World War II powers are comfortably ensconced atop the Security Council in New York, emerging and middle powers demand greater representation. Where a universal set of economic rules nominally has broad support, the WTO is buckling under pressure from closed economies and procedural atrophy. And where American primacy is clearly waning as a pillar of global order, each major power has distinct preferences for the international configuration that should replace it. Meanwhile, ungoverned spaces are more expansive, complex, and consequential as technology advances and the post–Cold War system becomes less capable of managing transnational challenges. No single universal vision of order will prevail in taming this unruly world—yet abject disorder need not be the unhappy fate.

As the United States prepares to pioneer its own vision for international strategy and order, it must consider the strategic landscape. Such a survey should go beyond crude assessments of regime type; while a state's internal sociopolitical organization provides some insight into its international behavior, the two are not identical. Where the contest for twenty-first-century order is most intense—on matters of economics and technology—the world is not cleanly divided according to autocracies versus democracies. As an authoritarian nation with extensive state intervention into its economy and society, China is highly unlikely to adopt major reforms, though it retains an overriding interest in brisk international trade. Russia faces greater incentives to hive itself off from the global economy, given its fear of financial coercion. Among the world's largest democracies, India is torn between liberal impulses toward economic and technological exchange and the expediency of protectionism and domestic repression in its quest for rapid development. Germany and Japan are far clearer in their commitment to interdependence—but the United States' own dalliance with trade wars demonstrates how even liberal democracies can undermine open systems.

But just as it would be a mistake to assume the "free world" stands lashed together in support of any one concept, we must not overlook potential for cooperation with illiberal and mixed-regime states as their individual strategies allow—particularly in the service of a twenty-first-century order that is multilayered and differentiated by issue, region, and domain in a manner that continues to serve American interests. Despite its authoritarianism, China has much to gain from climate cooperation; so too would it benefit from regimes that enable coexistence in space and effective management of global pandemics. Russia will continue to be a necessary partner on arms control and nonproliferation if the world's deadliest weapons are to remain unused. And, as India and Japan have recognized, cooperation with rapidly growing Asian states— especially mixed regimes in Southeast Asia—will be the most effective bulwark against a Chinese sphere of influence in that region. Forswearing any such cooperation would be a grievous error. So too would it be a mistake for Washington to assume that Moscow and Beijing's shared illiberal tendencies are sufficient grounds for an enduring alliance, despite a deep history of rivalry and already-apparent tensions over both nations' ambitions in Central Asia.

Even so, in a world of fluid alignments and contests for the allegiances of small and middle powers alike, the United States will gain tremendous advantage if it can count on the stalwart support of democratic partners like Japan and Germany. With these states, alignment on a common vision—and a plan for its realization on the basis of each ally's comparative advantages—will be paramount. Even if un- or partially democratic regimes do not come along, such alignments can prevent antithetical forms of order from crystallizing.

Finally, India clearly stands apart as a hinge state with unsettled preferences and extraordinary influence over the future of global as well as regional order. Its strategy to date belies hope that the United States could win its unconditional alignment as a counterbalance to China regionally and in favor of its preferred vision of order internationally. Moreover, its development trajectory suggests domestic concerns will remain primary over the coming decade. Nevertheless, American strategists should consider the future of order with India in mind. Cleaving Delhi from Beijing on issues of trade nondiscrimination, technological governance, and climate change are the highest priorities. The United States should be willing to accede to some of India's demands for procedural reform—or at least elevate them to the point where Chinese and Russian obstructionism becomes painfully obvious—in exchange for cooperation on matters of order renovation and construction that may ultimately allow the international system to remain fluid and accessible. Washington will not win the contest for twenty-first-century order if it cannot stave off forces of closure and keep the international system open.

FIVE

Toward an Open World

Although the United States will not be able to set the terms of twenty-first-century international order unilaterally, it must lead with a clear vision of the system it seeks to create. That vision must be guided, first and foremost, by an effort to secure the country's most vital national interests. As it has in the past, U.S. grand strategy must advance American security and prosperity, but the terms with which those are defined have evolved along with the order itself.

American national security has long been understood as the country's ability to prevent attacks on the homeland, or on U.S. populations living overseas. In a world of energetic nonmilitary competition, however, American foreign policy must also parry other threats against the country's political independence: cyber attacks, democratic interference, and major political, economic, or technological forms of subversion that have military-like consequences or impair vital domestic functions.

American foreign policy must also advance the country's prosperity. Prosperity is multidimensional, but best understood in aggregate terms as continual growth in national wealth that redounds to the benefit of all Americans. In twenty-first-century terms, growth rests upon a foundation of long-term economic competitiveness. Such competitiveness will rely upon effective technological exploitation, not only as a matter of national productivity but also as an essential export; it will also require mitigating structural disparities that undermine the United States' unity and economic vitality. Redistribution is therefore an essential element of a complementary domestic policy agenda that confronts inequality directly.

To advance its security and prosperity in the world it will meet, the United States must pursue a strategy founded on the concept of global openness. An openness strategy will represent a clear departure from grand strategies of the past, as well as their most prominent alternatives. It recognizes that Washington cannot hope to return to post–Cold War liberal internationalism, which aspired to a near-teleological convergence among democratic and authoritarian regimes; it should not seek to retrench from the world in part or whole; nor can it presume to contain its clearest competitor, or to prosecute competition along solely ideological lines.

Instead, a forward-looking American strategy should seek an international system that is itself open, and that promotes interstate interactions of the same quality. An ideal order will be populated by politically independent states and characterized by accessible global commons. This would be a world in which no competitor establishes a closed bloc and one that remains connected and interdependent. The U.S. strategy must strive for international transparency and good governance. It should posit that domestic regime preferences do not fully determine a state's international behavior, and accept the need to cooperate occasionally with illiberal states as mutual interest dictates, acknowledging that international order will increasingly be multilayered and differentiated. In this world, the United States must act to ensure that existing institutions support openness, and to build necessary rules and regimes in its service. Most taxing in Asia and least ambitious in the Middle East, an openness strategy has distinct regional requirements and burdens. Above all, it recognizes that the United States does not possess nor does it require strategic primacy to guarantee its security and prosperity, so long as it proceeds with a clear-eyed vision of the world it faces.

American History and Open Worlds

The search for an open world is hardly a new quest in American strategy; openness has a venerable national history. Since at least the late nineteenth century, the United States has sought to prevent a hegemonic adversary or bloc from controlling Europe, Asia, or both. If a competitor came to dominate hierarchically part or all of Eurasia in a manner that displaced U.S. political, economic, or military power, this strategic logic holds, it could expose the United States to direct threats to its prosperity and national security and, by extension, to domestic freedom.[1] Initial iterations of openness were pragmatic antidotes to early twentieth-century unilateralism and disengagement, codified in postwar institutions, although the concept did not ultimately survive rivalry with the Soviet Union and the structural constraints of the Cold War. In the twenty-first century, however, openness holds new promise as a vision that can guarantee a secure and prosperous world, despite the twilight of American unipolarity.

During the Second World War, American policymakers, led by President Franklin Roosevelt, sought a new grand strategic concept that would avert the failings of the First World War settlement and steer the world away from economic collapse and renewed conflict. "Openness" became a descriptor associated with sustained American international engagement. The concept recognized a preference for democracy, a liberal system of trade and commerce, and governance by multilateral institutions. In FDR's vision, an open order would reflect the Atlantic Charter's emphasis on political self-determination, and would be enforced by the United

Nations and buttressed by the General Agreement on Tariffs and Trade (GATT, later the WTO). Indeed, in this early American conception, seminal postwar institutions were constructed with the express purpose of promoting an open world and preventing great-power spheres of influence.[2]

Roosevelt's vision of openness did not survive him. Even before the war concluded, analysts and policymakers understood that the Soviet Union would have a postwar sphere of influence in some form. FDR acknowledged this fact at the 1943 Tehran Conference; as the war wound down, Soviet influence "east of the Elbe" was strongly presumed. In this transitional period, American opposition to spheres of influence was "conditional, not categorical"—for a time, U.S. strategists were comfortable with the idea of the Soviet Union having an "open" sphere. Soviet regional arrangements would nonetheless be porous to outside economic interests and would not threaten the military security of the United States and its partners. So long as Soviet client states were allowed to participate in international agreements and develop their own economies, Soviet influence was not necessarily grievous. This conception of an "open" sphere assumed fairly benign intentions from the Soviet Union, and was deemed to be acceptable, whereas "exclusive" spheres were not.[3]

Post-1945 realities dashed openness as a strategic objective. Once American policymakers believed the Soviet Union was seeking to subjugate Eastern Europe, they could no longer trust Moscow to build a sphere that was permeable and therefore tolerable. They increasingly understood that power and governance would be segmented into "two worlds," and that they could determine the nature of governance in theirs alone. Containment did not countenance but did acknowledge the fact that a hostile Soviet sphere would likely exist until the system collapsed under its own weight; in the interim, the United States would promote its strategic objectives within its own sphere. The United States had to settle for openness in the "free world," where its aspirations to political, economic, and security access became additional forms of liberal order.[4]

The Soviet sphere broke only with the end of the Cold War, when American aspirations surged to fill the space. During the unipolar period, there was no obvious reason why Washington could not hope for and work toward liberal universalism—no rival was capable of constructing a genuine alternative.

American primacy was always likely to be a happy but transitory circumstance; with its passing, U.S. strategists must grapple with how the country can guarantee its security and prosperity with something less than unrivaled power. The challenge is all the greater given that America's present-day rivals are authoritarian countries that may again seek to fashion the closed spheres that U.S. strategists have long deemed inimical, though only China has the means to accomplish the task. Policymakers must revive the concept of openness to govern a more constrained world in which American interests cannot be guaranteed.

In the twenty-first century, openness should characterize both American strategic priorities and the types of interactions the United States will facilitate in their service. An open international system is one in which all states have political and economic freedom of action and can make independent strategic decisions without being forced into closed blocs or camps that could result in their hierarchical dominance by more powerful states. So too must the global commons remain open, essential as they are to power projection by the U.S. military, international commerce, and the exchange of people and ideas. Openness favors sustained interstate cooperation, beneficial trade, and the free flow of information across borders to the greatest extent possible. It also calls for transparent governance within international institutions—even when participants are not themselves full-fledged democracies.

Crucial changes in international politics mean that twenty-first-century openness may be easier to obtain than a similar concept was in the mid-twentieth century. Modern openness does not assume benign great-power intentions—for example, by accepting a Chinese sphere with the hope that Beijing will consent to keep it open. Rather, it hedges against contrary competitor aspirations and relies on the fact that the terms of great-power politics have changed in ways that make openness more feasible to secure. Where the Soviet Union established a geographic bloc proximate to its borders, twenty-first-century great powers will measure their influence largely in economic and technological terms. Globalization enables states to benefit from each other's markets, technological bases, and industrial capacities without territorial conquest and consequent burdens of occupation. What is more, economic interdependence increases the costs of closure, as shuttered societies and markets cannot benefit from network effects, growth at a global scale, or efficiencies engendered by specialization. And while it is hardly impossible that any great power will make an explicit hegemonic bid through the use of force, a host of postwar factors, including international law and institutions, norms against conquest, and the proliferation of nuclear weapons, render that scenario unlikely (with the possible exception of a Chinese invasion of Taiwan). Ultimately, where geography is less relevant, force less potent, and commerce and information ever more important, it is more difficult and less advantageous for rivals to engineer the wholesale exclusion of the United States and like-minded countries. To guarantee that they do not, however, the United States must have a clear-eyed view of the requirements of openness in a contested world.[5]

Combating Closure

Consistent with historical approaches, openness stands in contrast to closed or hierarchical spheres of influence. In a closed sphere, outside political, economic, and security influence is blunted due to a hegemon's exercise of top-down control—as in the Soviet bloc during the Cold War. Interstate interactions are made under the shadow of great-power dominance, whether formalized in coercive rules or conducted informally through power-based hierarchy. An openness strategy seeks to prevent hostile powers from exercising hierarchical economic, political, or military control over geographic regions, subregions, or functional areas.

Openness begins by confronting the possibility that a great-power rival may seek to dominate a regional sphere. Although great powers face disincentives and practical barriers to the establishment of shuttered spheres, it is nonetheless possible that rivals could use territorial seizure or military intervention to assert hierarchical dominance over a geographic area.

Contemporary spheres of influence, however, may manifest in novel ways, with readily identifiable features. Interstate interactions would be antithetical to openness if powerful states were to directly subvert the domestic-political processes of weaker states—whether through cyber meddling in elections, subornment of local governance, or covert operations to neutralize or infiltrate political groups. Foreign-built infrastructure projects may allow great powers to compromise others' political independence through opaque lending terms and poor governance, and compulsory changes or suspensions of local laws and regulations. Construction of digital infrastructure, like 5G networks, may present novel opportunities for more powerful states to undermine their targets' sovereignty by brazenly curtailing access to telecommunications networks or more subtly using inappropriately obtained data, covert or overt censorship, and surveillance that violates domestic law. Future spheres may therefore depart from their historically geographic parameters, instead manifesting in functional domains and encompassing noncontiguous states across regions.

Interactions of these types could ultimately cumulate in a world of spheres dominated by regional hegemons. In its more extreme instantiation, a partitioned world would entail blocs of states under quasi-imperial control by a metropole in Beijing or Moscow, with various local governing structures. For reasons enumerated above, the costs of armed empire building would seem to outweigh the benefits—though softer forms of imperium by consent or acquiescence, induced by extravagant economic incentives and AI-enabled surveillance systems, may prove more feasible.[6] Such twenty-first-century blocs would be characterized by segmented information environments, whereby states living under authoritarian hegemons operate within a balkanized internet that affords less privacy, greater surveillance, and restricted access to information. They may also feature neo-mercantilist trading systems whereby peripheral states provide both raw materials and export markets for the dominant power, with blocs operating under centrally directed rules governing issues such as the state's role in markets, intellectual property protection, and terms of economic cooperation with external states or companies. A dominated sphere would be in the offing if great powers began to restrict free movement, as protected by international law, in the sea, air, or outer space—for example, if China curtailed the U.S. military's ability to fly, sail, and operate within the First Island Chain or denied commercial space activity through the employment of anti-satellite weapons.

An openness strategy does not preclude other major powers from garnering considerable regional influence. Indeed, China has already reestablished itself as a regional power, and attempting to dislodge its influence in Southeast Asia is a dubious charge. Instead, openness dictates that no rival should itself exclude American political, economic, and security power. Such a strategy does not require states to choose between dueling camps or blocs—aligning, for example, with Washington or Beijing. Indeed, openness prefers that states reject any temptation toward hierarchy in favor of a dynamic system in which blocs are taxing to establish. Although an openness strategy does not require American military primacy, it does necessitate sufficient political, economic, and military power to deter rivals, convincing them of the impossibility of establishing closed zones at tolerable costs. Diplomatic power will rise in importance as continually shifting, issue-specific alignments demand persistent American engagement focused on understanding regional states' interests and attracting their support, and nonmilitary competition intensifies. Unlike strategies that are prepared to cede a contemporary sphere of influence to Beijing, therefore, openness acknowledges the inevitable rise of Chinese power, but insists that influence not come at the price of American geographic or functional exclusion.[7] Russia, by contrast, has less potential for regional influence even as it has proved far more tolerant of risks in its attempts to delineate an exclusive local sphere. Moscow has already demonstrated an interest in limited territorial conquest in Crimea, Eastern Ukraine, and Georgia and, amid a push toward autarky, is less restrained by benefits accrued through participation in global commerce. Yet long-term power trends suggest that Moscow does not have the capacity to establish a closed regional sphere by coercive means, and its spoilerism will primarily aim to undermine EU and NATO unity without building real alternatives. If Russia continues attempting to expand its sphere by cleaving slices of its near abroad from the West, these gains may be symbolically grave, but they are unlikely to encompass a significant swath of Eurasia.

Openness does not, of course, incorporate the totality of American strategic objectives. Other threats, like nuclear proliferation, disease, or terrorism, may menace vital U.S. interests. Yet closed spheres of influence—whether exercised regionally or in particular domains—present the greatest danger to the United States' security and prosperity. A world in which American companies compete freely and fairly around the world, domestic industries and consumers benefit from participation in an international supply chain, the U.S. military enjoys unhindered access to the global commons, and information flows freely through digital pipelines is one in which American national security and economic well-being are best preserved. As an exceptionally powerful nation, the United States stands alone in its ability to combat closure and, without openness, few other U.S. aims can be guaranteed. Yet even as an openness vision embraces the benefits of interdependence, it also recognizes the reality of negative externalities. It accepts that a closed international system might better contain the spread of some transnational challenges but calculates that state-based threats are more consequential. Many transnational challenges, moreover, are more amenable to management via multilateral cooperation, even among geopolitical rivals. Furthermore, openness allows space for domestic policies that rely on some form of national closure; for openness to succeed as an international ordering principle, states need not abandon their borders or sovereignty to unrestricted migration or unfettered capital flows, for example.

Openness Objectives

To prevent a closed world from materializing, an openness strategy must adopt several interlocking objectives. First, openness relies on the political independence of states in the international system. If states in a given region, subregion, or functional system lose the ability to make free economic, political, and security choices, a closed sphere of influence would result. A rival could also formalize efforts to shutter a sphere in the shape of an international institution or regime that is governed autocratically, thereby limiting participating states' choices and freedom of action. The central strategic objective of openness is to prevent such an outcome in the form of a power-based hierarchy or formal governance structure, guaranteeing that states retain self-determination in their interstate interactions. It does not, however, extend to individual liberties, as openness is a model for international, not domestic, governance.

Second, to prevent closed spheres, American strategy must preserve open access to the global commons. Without establishing a hierarchy that co-opts sovereign countries, a rival could nonetheless obtain a shuttered sphere or otherwise disrupt global openness if it closed off sea, air, or space to other countries, preventing the free operations to which all are entitled under international law. Any scheme that requires advance notification and permission to transit areas outside internationally recognized territorial boundaries—whether air defense identification zones, illegal search or seizure of ships, or nationally imposed tolls—would imperil free access to the global commons. The United States and its allies must therefore uphold freedom of navigation in sea and airspace, as guaranteed under the UN Convention on the Law of the Sea, as well as in space, in accordance with the Outer Space Treaty and other governing instruments. According to interpretations of UNCLOS held by much of the world, international law guarantees these freedoms to commercial and military vessels alike, and does not require transiting states to give notification to or receive permission from the coastal state in question.[8] If and when states systematically violate laws applying to the seas and air, or use the threat of military force to close the commons, Washington and its allies must strenuously oppose them. In space, openness precludes malicious or irresponsible activity that renders it an unsafe operating environment for commercial, scientific, or military craft—such as debris-producing anti-satellite tests or refusal to adhere to internationally agreed launch notification procedures.

Third, a sound strategy must ensure that existing international institutions are reflective of openness in their form and function—an objective that will require reform to some long-standing bodies. While most leading states continue to support the UN as the system's governing political body and the organization remains effective, many also agree that Security Council membership is a vestige of the postwar era. The basic principles of openness are reflected in the UN Charter itself, but to ensure that the body remains a buttress to political openness as international power shifts, the United

States should support reform proposals that improve UNSC representation. Moreover, the World Trade Organization has ground to a standstill because its rules were not written for nonmarket economies. Nonmarket countries systematically fail to disclose subsidies and other state-directed practices, and have capitalized on these gaps. By maintaining closed economies while participating in international bodies, they exploit the openness of the international trading regime.

Fourth, openness will require that the United States and its partners build new rules and institutions in undergoverned spaces, lest rivals shape these domains in ways that result in closure. Nondemocratic states' preference for walled information systems means their preferred forms of internet governance will not be acceptable to Washington and its partners, for example. Rather than wait for problematic norms to crystallize, the United States should craft its own regimes in contentious areas like the internet, cyberspace, and AI, expecting its rivals will not subscribe but welcoming their partial participation if they so choose. While Washington may not be able to prevent the emergence of a splinternet, it can ensure that Russia and China's preferred norms like cyber sovereignty are not ratified by international institutions like the UN.

In select areas of order building, an openness strategy may entail robust cooperation with illiberal rivals to address transnational challenges. Climate change and migration present two such opportunities, so long as regimes are crafted transparently. Particularly as China grows increasingly active in the development space, the United States can collaborate with Beijing to direct additional resources toward climate mitigation and adaptation-focused projects, and to ensure all infrastructure development efforts are environmentally sustainable. Where the United States and China do cooperate, however, they will do so on the basis of issue-specific interest convergence rather than as a result of any type of "G2" or grand bargain arrangement. In an increasingly dynamic and multipolar world in which China may selectively favor closure, a great power condominium is unlikely to be feasible or desirable for the United States.

Fifth, the United States should support existing democracies, encouraging democratic consolidation and assisting their defense against threats to political independence. The United States benefits from acting as a liberal power—both at home and abroad—so that the virtues of operating in a U.S.-led system remain evident to other states, but Washington need not change the internal character of states to guarantee openness across regions and functional domains because regime type is not strictly determinative of a state's ability to participate in open governance. Nevertheless, democracies are far likelier than other regime types to align with openness principles, and an open international system will fare better if the United States uses economic and political power to bolster liberal states that are experiencing notable backsliding.

Thus, despite the United States' preference for democratic partners, an openness strategy departs from past efforts at regime change, which have repeatedly proven to be exceptionally difficult, costly, and rife with unintended consequences. Humility about the United States' ability to influence domestic outcomes in authoritarian states is not tantamount to agnosticism, however; Washington should continue to support democracy rhetorically, calling attention to repressive domestic closure, including human rights abuses, through existing international laws and institutions that respect other countries' political independence. Materially, however, it should focus its aid efforts on supporting those countries in which procedural elements of democracy remain, using its resources to backstop democracy where its institutional components can be salvaged and buttressed.

An openness-based strategy represents a clear departure from the principles of liberal internationalism that have guided U.S. strategy since the end of the Cold War—particularly, its increasingly elusive quest to recoup American military primacy.[9] Instead of presuming the eventual triumph of liberalism, openness acknowledges the lamentable fact that the United States will have to live alongside illiberal states until their people choose otherwise. While the liberal international order was never a monolithic set of structures or a coherent agenda, it represented an aspirational set of principles whose universalist claims are now hotly contested. In particular, geopolitical actors of significant import will not strive for ever-freer markets or hold preferences for liberal democracy. Indeed, Russia and China will seek to attenuate those principles through disruption and transformation, respectively, making primacy difficult to recoup.

U.S. policymakers must not only abandon their assumptions that much of the world is moving toward teleological economic and political end states; they must assume that competitors who seek to divert from them are largely ensconced in existing forms of order, and will build novel ordering concepts of their own. An openness strategy anticipates a world in which the United States does not monopolize the ability to construct new rules and regimes; rather, it expects other powerful actors to proffer new institutions, even as Washington and its partners try to preserve existing bodies and to establish new openness-based rules of their own.

This pluralism does not mean, however, that the United States should adopt a restrained, offshore posture, empowering regional states to self-defend and potentially ceding large swaths of geographic or functional space to Russia and China.[10] To do so would be to accept a world governed along illiberal lines. Instead, openness is a strategic objective that requires substantial, if transformed, global engagement. By emphasizing openness in international governance, it expects flexibility and access even in those parts of the world where authoritarian competitors—namely, China—have greater institutional influence. International order will thus become increasingly multilayered and differentiated: functionally, it will encompass an eclectic array of institutions, norms, and laws;

structurally, it will range in formality from legalized institutions to informal processes based on interest convergence; and geographically, it will contain global, regional, and subregional bodies. Longstanding institutions will thus endure alongside diverse new regimes.[11]

An openness strategy also departs from "free world" or neocontainment strategies that anticipate a world divided along democratic versus authoritarian lines.[12] Instead, it assumes there is an imperfect correlation between the domestic character of a regime and its international governance. That is, autocratic and mixed-regime states may nonetheless be willing to exercise transparency and good governance in international institutions and regimes, uphold free access to the global commons, engage in rule-based cross-border commerce, or cooperate to address climate change. It is not, therefore, to U.S. advantage to simply refuse to work with mixed regimes, or even occasionally with illiberal states, as interests align. If the United States crafts a strategy that relies on democracies alone, it leaves mixed regimes to align with its authoritarian rivals, creating dominated spheres by default. If, instead, it supposes that regime type is not fully determinative of international behavior, and works to promote transparency and international governance for all states on the international level, the United States will deny ideologically based closure and expand the potential zone of openness. Openness does not require that American foreign policy seek to change the internal character of individual states for it to obtain on an international level.

Openness by Region

Despite its unifying principles, an openness strategy will have distinct objectives and approaches in each major region. This variation can be explained primarily by the risk that a hostile actor will be able to establish a closed sphere, and by the extent of U.S. interests that would be jeopardized by such a hierarchy. Openness is a global strategy, but one whose resources are concentrated where threats to closure are most grave. In the effort to achieve openness, the strategic burden on the United States is by far the most onerous in Asia, can be realized by supporting allies in Europe, and is least pressing in the Middle East. These relative risks and stressors call for a foreign policy that allocates significant military, diplomatic, and economic resources to Asia; sustained but secondary military support to Europe, alongside deep diplomatic engagement; and a relatively light military footprint in the Middle East, coupled with a continued diplomatic and economic presence. In Africa and the Western Hemisphere, American engagement will rely primarily on nonmilitary tools. Threats to openness will not, however, be cleanly bounded by geography, and resisting closure in order's diverse components will require distinctly tailored means. A regional survey nevertheless elucidates the relative priorities of an openness strategy.

Asia

The most obvious threat to global openness is China's continued ascent in Asia: of all U.S. rivals, only Beijing may have the will and ability to design an exclusive regional sphere that expels American power, jeopardizes states' political independence, or closes the global commons. Under these conditions, the United States would be less able to guarantee its security and prosperity, as the interdependence on which it has long relied would be imperiled. Since the 2008 financial crisis and Xi Jinping's 2012–13 ascent, the CCP has been explicit about its goal of reestablishing regional hegemony in Asia by 2021 and of climbing to the status of global superpower by midcentury. In these dual objectives of regional hegemony and global power status, China has distinguished itself as one of the more transparent great powers in history. The party has also identified some general requirements of those strategic conditions, including the mitigation of American power in Asia, a restoration of significant regional influence, and the reestablishment of control over disputed territories, although many of its objectives remain undefined.[13]

Furthermore, as China's ascent has continued, the CCP has undeniably become more authoritarian at home. Xi's domestic measures include an even stronger role for the government in the Chinese economy, the systematic internment of ethnic minorities, the manufacture of a sophisticated surveillance state with a closed internet at its core, and the abolition of the notion of collective leadership in favor of Xi's permanent installation. At present, there is no indication that the Chinese intend to change their political system. Xi's preference for a closed Chinese information environment already has a foreign policy analogue in China's support of techno-authoritarianism. Although a state's domestic regime preferences do not neatly predict its international governance tendencies, China's digital surveillance is an example of a clear connection.[14]

American analysts cannot presume that China's global ascent will proceed in a linear or irreversible direction. Nor does the United States possess the ability to upend China's growth trajectory, military spending, stated strategic objectives, or domestic system. For the time being, then, American strategists must devise an approach that allows the United States to live with and protect vital interests from an authoritarian near-peer in Asia. American strategy must hedge against the possibility that China's regional aspirations are fundamentally irreconcilable with openness.

The United States cannot avoid a stronger China able to exert significant regional influence, but it can seek to prevent China from establishing a dominant sphere of influence—a bloc that would allow it to suborn part or all of Asia in a manner that displaces U.S. political, economic, or military power. An exclusive zone could leave the United States unable to access vital markets and strip it of its forward defensive position, thereby breaking alliance commitments, undermining the U.S. military's ability to enforce openness of the regional commons, and ultimately jeopardizing American prosperity and national security. Although contemporary Chinese hegemony will not replicate that of the USSR in its Eastern European sphere, the central geopolitical concern of Cold War strategists remains paramount: the United States should seek to avert the domination of any swath of Eurasia by a hostile rival.[15]

The positive objective of U.S. strategy should therefore be an open Asia. An open Asia is one in which regional states have political and economic freedom of action and are able to make independent strategic decisions without being forced into closed blocs or camps that could result in their hierarchical control. Under this concept, Asia's commons must also remain accessible, essential as they are to international commerce and military transit. Openness favors beneficial trade and the free flow of information across borders. It also calls for transparent international governance, particularly in regional institutions that China itself may lead.

An openness strategy rejects the notion that regional states should "choose" between the United States and China and instead incentivizes them to eschew great-power dominance in favor of agency. Particularly given the emergence of regional economic multipolarity in the coming decade, an openness strategy encourages strategic autonomy for middle powers. It accepts India, for example, as a wholly independent actor. Indeed, it seeks to buttress Delhi's ordering role as well as its relationship with Washington, knowing that openness will be far more attainable if India actively supports it. It also encourages independence and dynamism among the region's mixed regimes, like Vietnam, Singapore, and Thailand, seeking cooperation where possible. At a time when the CCP seeks a more closed Chinese society, commons, and global information space, the United States should strive to preserve the region's accessibility and fluidity. Of course, an Asia of dynamic alignments and enhanced middle-power agency implies the United States will sometimes lose the support of these hinge states on important matters of regional governance—but it also wagers that Asian states would ultimately prefer to live in an open region, backstopped by an American presence, rather than one characterized by Chinese hegemony. Openness supposes, therefore, that U.S. strategy can help to shape China's own order-building efforts in Asia, such that they may be moderately revisionist without being revolutionary.[16]

Openness in Asia will not be easily obtained. Regional openness requires that Asia be the United States' primary military theater but does not demand military primacy. While high-end deterrence remains essential, openness will not be guaranteed through military strategy alone. Indeed, China's regional and global objectives mean it should prefer to establish its sphere without triggering the conflict that could derail its rise. We should therefore expect China's regional expansion to continue to occur largely below the military threshold. Whether incursions come in the form of maritime grabs, cyber intrusions, stifling economic coercion, or information and influence campaigns, sub-conventional deterrence generally requires swift transparency, specific deterrent threats, clear messaging, and some tolerance for risk. The United States cannot seek to deter or prevent all Chinese coercion, but should focus on thwarting sub-conventional bids that may contribute to closed spheres, such as efforts to restrict freedom of navigation in the South China Sea.[17]

Openness in Asia also has complex nonmilitary requirements. Economic openness requires that the United States abandon reflexive protectionism and restore itself as a credible leader in the trading regime. Technological openness requires that Washington and its allies provide alternatives to closed and unreliable information systems and suggests that they must promote openness in undergoverned spaces to keep closed norms from crystallizing.[18] It implies that the same states should give infrastructure and development aid and make investments that promote transparency. Amid shifting relative power, it requires that the United States approach all of the foregoing in close coordination with its regional as well as European allies, without which it cannot maintain necessary balance. Most important, an openness strategy recognizes that Washington does not require unequivocal regional dominance to prevent China from establishing a hierarchy of its own—though an open order cannot be guaranteed without proactive American leadership.

Europe

A novel American strategy must also strive to keep Europe open and vibrant. Unlike China, Russia does not pose a fundamental threat to openness—Moscow may wish to establish a closed sphere, but it lacks the capability to do so. Yet, in a European openness strategy, Moscow is not the sole concern: the United States requires the cooperation of its European allies to secure openness in Asia too. As such, the United States can seek an open Europe by supporting highly capable allies as they improve their ability to deter and defend against high-end conflict, thwart Moscow's subconventional incursions, and avert democratic backsliding. Outside of the region, the United States will need its allies at the core of any alternative models of economic or technological governance. NATO must be the primary vehicle for all of these efforts.

Although Putin may long for the days when Russia had a sphere of influence in its near abroad, the country's trajectory is one of decline, and it will not have the means to build such a zone. Russia cannot engage in sustained peer competition with the United States, much less exercise power so formidable that it can exclude the United States from parts of the region. While it has some latitude for coercion, particularly of clients with few alternatives, like Ukraine, this reach is limited. Moscow will not boast Beijing's market size or state coffers for the next decade-plus, nor is it an engine of technological innovation. Even so, Russia has significant military capabilities in certain areas—particularly its nuclear arsenal—and the benefit of mass and proximity in Eastern Europe. These, in turn, could allow it to make a fait accompli seizure in the Baltics, forcing NATO to choose between acquiescence and potentially catastrophic escalation. More likely, however, Moscow will act as a sub-conventional spoiler, pursing election meddling, treaty violation, and foreign intervention to rattle the European security order. Yet Moscow's desire to be recognized as a great power does not bestow it with the vision or the ability to craft a new regional order. Its lackluster regional institutions betray its struggle to reestablish influence, let alone construct an exclusive sphere.

Without closing a sphere, however, Moscow can still menace European openness, as malign interstate interactions can threaten other states' domestic openness as well as their ability to participate in an open international system. Russia's interference in democratic processes is a threat to the political independence of European states, and its use of sub-conventional tactics has abetted democratic backsliding. Unlike in Asia, where the United States must devote considerable resources of its own to reinforce existing allies and build new partnerships against a shifting power balance, trend lines in Europe are more favorable. European allies can hold the front lines of regional openness if they have sufficient support. European GDP and military spending compare favorably to Russia's, particularly when pooled together, so the United States should buttress its allies as they contain these threats to openness. First, to help deter and defend in high-end conflict, the United States should emphasize NATO partner contributions and training to improve allied readiness. It should also work closely with NATO allies to confront Russian threats at the sub-conventional level, even as European partners take primary responsibility for incursions against their own states. Finally, it should support allies to ensure that European openness does not degrade from within by monitoring democratic backsliding and providing democracy support within the alliance and along its periphery. Russian revanchism will continue to pose a significant challenge to Europe and its security order; it will not, however, amount to a closed sphere.

The shifting balance of power in Asia demands the strategic focus of European allies as well. While the United States should not expect its European partners to make major military contributions to keeping Asia open, all will have to work together to reinforce essential elements of regional order. They must coordinate their approaches to BRI, advocating for better governance and developing alternatives in tandem; build an open future for cyber security and internet governance in lockstep; continue to support the primacy of international law in the global commons; collaborate on international strategies for addressing nonmilitary coercion, particularly when it imperils political independence; and, most important, align their long-term strategies for an open Europe and Asia as critical components of a shared global vision.

Middle East

In the Middle East, the United States cannot hope to secure openness of the type it seeks in Asia and Europe. Although the region will not become a closed sphere of influence, it will remain highly disordered. To the extent that domestic openness penetrates the region, its reach will be limited by regional rivalries, great-power interference, and civil strife. An openness strategy must work to ensure that a volatile Middle East does not become a threat to openness elsewhere via destabilizing exports of terrorism or migrants, while also preserving free maritime commons in the region's strategically vital waterways. Precisely because of the enormous difficulty of establishing regional control for any state—whether a regional power or a global one—an openness strategy can permit additional great-power involvement in regional governance, including economic development projects, freedom of navigation missions, nonproliferation efforts, and multilateral management of migration flows. As the United States' lamentably precipitous withdrawal from Syria has demonstrated, American drawdown may benefit other great powers without necessarily abetting their dominance.

Terrorism and migration, moreover, may result in threats to global openness elsewhere. While an openness strategy cannot hope to wholly eliminate the terrorist threat, it must ensure that the Middle East cannot become a base for attacks on the American homeland or troops stationed overseas. Such an end state does not require a peaceful and democratic region, and it may entail cooperation with some decidedly unsavory local partners in the broader service of an open international system. Amid ongoing civil conflict—exacerbated by the effects of climate change—migration will continue to tax international capacity for the absorption of displaced persons. An openness strategy should seek new multilateral arrangements to manage this challenge.

The core openness principle at greatest risk in the Middle East is freedom of navigation. Openness of the global commons will require that Iranian threats to shipping in the Straits of Hormuz remain at bay, including through operations that contest Tehran's overly expansive interpretation of its rights to restrict navigation. Though not presently under threat, the Suez Canal must remain free and open. In the Horn of Africa, an openness strategy would seek to prevent piracy from endangering international commerce, expanding and further multilateralizing existing counter-piracy efforts, which already count the United States, the EU, NATO, China, India, and Russia as contributors.

With clear great-power threats in Asia and Europe, the United States will need to draw down its Middle East military presence. Enough capability must remain to defeat potential state or nonstate attacks on the homeland or U.S. bases, with persistent devotion of significant intelligence assets. The U.S. Navy should also continue missions in the global commons to promote freedom of navigation. Together, U.S. military and intelligence capabilities should be sufficient to provide "early warning" of regional threats that could directly menace the United States or its overseas interests.[19] While such a posture necessarily adopts more security risk, the United

States will remain deeply engaged in the region diplomatically and economically. It may even begin new initiatives, such as novel regimes to ensure that regional hurdles to global openness are co-operatively managed. Although Washington expects the region to remain disordered, Middle East turmoil may have some salutary effects: the United States will have relatively less influence than it has had for the last two decades, but it will be equally difficult for Russia or China to establish dominance.

The Western Hemisphere and Africa

Although openness is focused primarily on Asia, followed by Europe, it should also recognize the importance of the Western Hemisphere and Africa as battlegrounds where the United States must compete to shape the future of international order.

Openness in the Western Hemisphere will be a complex undertaking. Historical ties born of geographic proximity, regional organizations like the Washington-based Organization of American States, and economic integration through trade agreements such as the North American Free Trade Agreement (NAFTA) and the Central American Free Trade Agreement (CAFTA) all suggest the United States will remain the most influential of all the great powers in Latin America. Yet competitors are trying to increase their influence in the region as China makes economic overtures through BRI and Russia deepens its relationships with Cuba, Nicaragua, and—most significantly—Venezuela. Although the United States should seek to preserve its preponderant influence in the Western Hemisphere, the region will not be an exclusive American zone. Washington cannot stop China, Russia, and others from gaining political and economic footholds via trade and investment, nor can it prevent arms sales and other forms of military-to-military ties. If those activities portended regional, subregional, or functional dominance by China or Russia, however, they would be impermissible. Moreover, given the Western Hemisphere's geographic proximity, any foreign action or power accumulation with the potential to directly threaten the United States would require a strong response, even if broader regional openness is not immediately at risk.

An openness strategy aims to reinforce American influence in the Western Hemisphere and forestall other great powers from creating the conditions for hierarchy. Strategy in Latin America will rely primarily on diplomatic and economic tools, and an openness strategy sees significant opportunities to expand trade ties with economic partners like Mexico, promote good governance through investment, cooperatively manage shared challenges like migration, and lead development initiatives alongside like-minded partners in areas like 5G. Given its salience to American security and prosperity, the Western Hemisphere should be a priority region as the next administration crafts its response to BRI.

In Africa, democracy support has the potential to reap substantial dividends. The southern and western parts of the continent have seen democratic governments flourish, whereas Central and East Africa are backsliding.[20] Particularly as Chinese investment permeates, the United States has a role to play in ensuring alternative sources of high-standards infrastructure development while also providing transparency, accountability, and monitoring assistance to African states that accept Chinese investment. Finally, given the outsized impact of climate change on the region, an openness strategy can preempt future threats to openness by leading investment initiatives focused on climate adaptation.

Strategizing for an Open World

As policymakers begin to contemplate the virtues of openness, they must consider a defining question: how would U.S. foreign policy be different under this strategy? What policies and actions would the United States forgo if it chooses to pursue openness? An openness strategy represents a clear departure from defining foreign policies of the last three presidential administrations. The contrasts with George W. Bush and Donald Trump are readily apparent. Whereas Bush initially invaded Iraq over later-debunked concerns about weapons of mass destruction, the mission quickly expanded into an effort to unseat Saddam Hussein and remake Iraq into a democracy. An openness strategy unequivocally rejects armed regime change—instead embracing a humility about the United States' ability to transform other societies, moderation in the application of military force, and a preference for multilateral management of the international consequences of odious dictators' domestic behavior. The Trump administration, for its part, has undermined the dearest principles of openness by abetting Russian and other interference in American elections, denigrating international institutions like the UN and WTO, abdicating efforts at new international governance, relishing unilateral economic protectionism, eschewing the strategic role of allies, and threatening armed regime change in Iran and Venezuela.

An openness strategy comes closer to the policy of the Obama administration, but the two nevertheless part in significant ways. Because of the strategic weight openness places on Asia, two regional examples are particularly instructive. Under openness, the United States would not have opposed China's Asian Infrastructure Investment Bank or pressured its allies to abstain from joining the regional organization. Supposing that domestic authoritarianism does not necessarily beget a threatening institution, Washington would not have detracted from AIIB simply because it was led by China. Instead, it would have coordinated strategies with like-minded states to push China to govern its new bank transparently. Indeed, this is the approach American allies ultimately took, and in so doing they largely succeeded in ensuring good governance at the AIIB. An openness strategy would have placed the United States at the helm of that effort instead of on its sidelines.[21]

But openness would also have required the United States to take a much more proactive stance elsewhere in Asia, even at increased risk of escalation with Beijing. China's rapid-fire island building and militarization of the South China Sea constituted a manifest effort to close part of the global commons—and one that has changed the balance of power in the waterway for good. In 2014–16, the United States attempted to rally partners in Asia to build a diplomatic coalition against China, but its efforts petered out. Under openness, a competitor's gray zone and military efforts to close a strategic waterway would call for muscular action. An American approach to Chinese militarization could have relied on targeted sanctions as well as specific deterrent statements to Beijing, even if these put other forms of U.S.-China cooperation at risk. Tensions between Washington and Beijing would surely have spiked for a time, but the South China Sea might still be a truly open waterway today.[22]

In these departures from past policy, an openness strategy undeniably assumes additional geopolitical risk. By refusing to cede to China a closed geographic or functional sphere of influence, it necessarily accepts the likelihood of sustained friction between Washington and Beijing. The strategy acknowledges that the two major powers will compete in traditional areas, such as the military balance of power in the western Pacific, alongside new domains, like technological innovation, market penetration, and governance. In pursuing international openness, the United States assumes greater escalation risks than it would by simply permitting Chinese dominance in certain regional or functional areas. But such risk acceptance reflects the calculation that closed geographic or functional spheres of Chinese influence would be far costlier to American security and prosperity. Moreover, by setting strategic objectives with appeal to mixed regimes as well as democracies, an openness strategy is more likely to find a diverse coalition of supporters, reducing the costs of its implementation to the United States. Finally, by setting clear standards for international interactions and outcomes, openness increases China's incentives to channel its growing power in a manner that is broadly compliant.

Of course, openness has its own conceptual limits and represents a necessary but insufficient strategic objective for the United States. Washington cannot achieve security and prosperity in a world of closure, and if the United States does not itself work toward openness, no other global power will be able to secure it. But openness has frailties, will create negative externalities, and must be conceptually bounded. As with any order, American strategy must recognize the limits of interstate cooperation, identify where zero-sum competition will continue to exist, and prepare to defend national interests in those areas.

The basic principle of openness fails to address transnational challenges that may themselves be the product of openness. Migration and global pandemics, for example, transcend state bounds and will continue to require international management, but openness does not prescribe clear policy solutions. Indeed, some amount of closure at both the state and international levels is likely necessary to manage each. These must be understood as exceptions to be managed so that the system as a whole can hew to its strategic mandate.

The pursuit of openness may also create significant negative externalities. An open international trading system may result in unequal gains within states, for example; the open nature of the commons means that the costs of climate change are borne collectively. The latter case calls for new forms of global governance, the former for domestic policy that addresses inequality. An open, interdependent world will always come with costs, even if aggregate benefits outweigh them, and an openness strategy must permit international and state-level rejoinders. The proper response for mitigating inevitable negative consequences must be dictated by where the costs manifest.

Moreover, it would be naïve to expect the United States or any country to pursue openness at the expense of its vital interests. The liberal international order persisted despite illiberal behavior by its leading states; an open order should also be robust if powerful actors periodically violate its core principles when national security is at stake. The United States need not, for example, sit idly by as China builds a substantial military presence in Central America, leave its markets open to companies that provide inroads for foreign government intervention, or welcome unlimited quantities of immigrants across its borders. Yet in asserting these caveats—which are potentially quite capacious—policymakers must guard against rapid races to closure and weigh short-term concerns against long-term benefits of reciprocal openness. Where openness is at odds with vital national interests, some combination of international regimes and domestic policy can serve as recourse, reestablishing the necessary balance between openness and inter- as well as intrastate stability.

As the leading force for international openness, the United States accepts unique responsibilities. The magnitude of American power affords some space for hypocrisy, but it also spotlights the United States as a global exemplar of the international behavior that an openness strategy seeks. An open order cannot endure if Washington does not model openness and bolster, rather than undermine, it from within. Exercising strategic discipline—particularly in the employment of its most potent coercive tools, like military force and financial sanctions—will reinforce this leadership role, even if other great powers such as China do not demonstrate reciprocal forbearance. Indeed, Beijing may well claim national security exemptions to many features of an open international order, and the strategy described in this book intentionally hedges against that possibility. Just as the liberal international order was never wholly liberal, international, nor orderly—even though it featured each of these characteristics in meaningful measure—an open system will always be both aspirational and manifest.[23]

The imperfections of openness are, nevertheless, undeniable. The policymakers who implement it must work to anticipate gaps, mitigate externalities, and acknowledge clear exceptions. These frailties, however, must be compared to those that would accompany an alternative strategy. The liabilities of a retrenchment strategy, for example, would be measured in the United States' inability to effect political and economic change in areas of former influence. The drawbacks of a persistently liberal-universalist strategy would likely come in the form of overreach, as policymakers devote resources to reshaping states whose characters cannot be transformed in Washington. An ideologically based containment strategy, which would by default cede dominant spheres of influence to authoritarian competitors, would blunt American influence and access. The costs of openness must also be compared to a world in which the United States is guided by no grand strategy at all. The peril of such a world is not, as is so often argued, persistent and pervasive disorder. Rather, increasingly, the gravest danger is the rise of alternative forms of order that may not be consistent with American security and prosperity, or those of other states.

Moreover, openness is a strategy that suits the preferences of the American people. For all that foreign policy commentators bemoan a public seemingly eager to disengage from international affairs, data show the opposite: a citizenry willing to remain active in the global arena. The public supports a foreign policy in which the United States continues to lead the world but shares this responsibility more broadly. It is highly supportive of diplomatic engagement, including through alliances and multilateral institutions, but opposes armed regime change and is skeptical of entanglement in the Middle East. It increasingly sees China as the primary state-based challenger, although there is a partisan divide in this threat perception. Overall, however, the American public appears to favor a disciplined form of internationalism—a strategy that is more consistent with openness than with any of its clear alternatives.[24]

What openness demands, therefore, is a fundamental rearranging of American foreign policy. A new approach must emphasize

Asia as the region that could become an exclusive sphere, followed by Europe, where threats to political independence remain but structural trends are more favorable. Openness also requires a rebalancing of foreign policy tools, recognizing that many threats to political independence and the global commons will occur below the military threshold and in nondefense domains. It calls for unprecedented cooperation between allies in Europe and Asia; these will themselves provide needed ballasts to international openness in the face of assertive revisionist challenges. It merits a calculated approach to existing and new institutions, so that formalized cooperation is used to prevent, rather than to facilitate, closure. And while openness is a conscious move away from the universalist aspirations of post–Cold War liberalism, it is nonetheless highly ambitious in its aims. It acknowledges sundown on the unipolar era, but insists that the openness alternative does not countenance American retrenchment; it anticipates new foreign policy constraints, but recognizes that significant opportunities remain and can be exploited through alliances, institutions, and sound strategy. Above all, openness asserts that the United States does not require unrivaled military or geopolitical primacy to secure its dearest global objectives—so long as it undertakes a dramatic reordering of foreign policy equal to the task.

SIX

A Policy for the Day After

At present, the United States is ill equipped to implement a long-term, coherent, and complex global strategy. Where domestic unity is desperately needed, the American polity is riven by bitter partisanship; where the United States requires allies as closer partners in ordering coalitions, those ties are growing threadbare; and where global openness requires buttressing, Washington has too often aligned with forces of closure through capricious trade wars, short-sighted disengagement from international institutions, and undue deference to autocratic powers. Yet, for all that the Trump administration has pursued policies that undermine openness and exacerbate unfavorable trends, Trump himself is not responsible for the domestic and international upheavals shaping twenty-first-century international politics. The long-term structural shifts we have analyzed would have confronted any chief executive elected in November 2016. These forces will not abate when Trump leaves office; rather, they represent the fundamental strategic challenges that a post-Trump presidency must confront.

In crafting a new American strategy for international order—one that both corrects for Trump's missteps and charts a novel course for the nation suitable to the world as it will be—the United States must begin with an openness-based approach. An openness strategy seeks to prevent closed spheres of influence, maintain free access to the global commons, defend the political independence of all states, modernize existing institutions, and build new forms of order. These principles do not alone offer a template for governance, however, and even the soundest of strategic concepts often founders in implementation. For openness to become the guiding principle for American foreign policy, therefore, the next administration must pursue an interlocking set of policy initiatives to build an open world.

It is urgent that global openness become the touchstone of U.S. foreign policy, but this will not easily be obtained. In its quest for openness, the greatest challenges to the United States are domestic: a new administration must strive to mend the chasm between the government and the tech sector to harness innovation for national advantage; it must also salvage U.S. foreign policy from the grips of political polarization. It must prepare for twenty-first-century international competition by recognizing that much of this competition will be nonmilitary in nature, and empower the State Department, focus the Pentagon, coordinate the national security bureaucracy, modernize the role of intelligence, and partner closely with allies as well as the private sector to prepare for it. Global openness will also require Washington to adopt new strategies for international order. It will need to build new forms of order in undergoverned spaces, including the internet, cyber, AI, trade, migration, and climate, lest others set new rules that will lead to international closure. It will also need to modernize existing institutions, including the UN Security Council and the WTO, to enhance their resilience to international change. Since novel American-led structures will not win universal adherence, Washington can prevent rival institutions from becoming insidious forces for closure by insisting on transparency and accountability as basic standards for all international governance.

The United States' ability to act as a force for global openness will depend fundamentally on its capacity to harness the private sector for national advantage. Pressures of competition with nonmarket economies will suffuse the contest for twenty-first-century order, but Washington should not seek to emulate state-led economies. Instead, it must pursue a new and distinctly American model of public-private partnership that protects the innovation and investment catalyzed by market forces while also directing corporate dynamism toward shared national objectives. With substantial legal, regulatory, political, and financial power to shape business incentives, the next administration must use its authority to align the private sector with foreign policy on a scale not seen in decades. A sustained, multidimensional approach to fostering such alignment will help openness prevail when faced with inevitable headwinds, whether partisan whiplash or technological change that rapidly outpaces regulation. To fully reap these gains, a new administration must also modernize government to seize upon commercial innovation for national security purposes.

For all that this agenda is Herculean and will take years to implement, the task could not be more urgent: if the United States fails to chart a course that accounts for these epochally transformative forces, it will find itself with a foreign policy utterly mismatched to the world it is facing—and Washington's power and influence will wane, when they might have remained formidable for decades to come.

Building Strength at Home

Of the challenges facing the United States over the next ten to fifteen years, the greatest come from within. To bolster the foundations of national power over the long term, the next administration must reinvest in the American people, American economy, and American democracy. Demographically, one of the United States' greatest assets is its ability to attract high-skilled and hard-working immigrants from around the globe; a sound immigration policy will help the United States seize this competitive advantage. Investments in healthcare and education—K-12, higher, civics, and STEM—will help to protect the enormous human capital advantages that the United States currently enjoys over its near-peer China. Economically, the United States remains a financial and innovation powerhouse, but long-term prosperity requires major investments in infrastructure, both in physical assets like roads and airports and digital projects like 5G networks; embrace of a green economy to generate jobs and make the United States a leader in green manufacturing; and serious measures to tackle economic inequality. Growth, productivity, and innovation are at the core of American power, and the next administration neglects structural reforms at its peril.[1]

Many of these investments extend far beyond the traditional scope of foreign policy. But to pursue a strategy of openness, the United States must retain its position as the world's mightiest nation, even if its margin of power diminishes in relative terms. It also must regain its strategic competency and preserve sufficient unity to prevent domestic instability from eclipsing global imperatives. Achieving these ends will require Washington to realign the tech sector and the national interest via new forms of public-private partnership alongside significant governmental investment in research and development, and to strengthen the basic foundations of American innovation. Successful policy also calls for steps to insulate foreign policy from political polarization, fostering a renewed sense of common national purpose.

The Tech Sector and the National Interest
At home, the next administration must find a model of public-private partnership that harnesses and extends America's innovative edge for national benefit. This requires Washington to reconceive of the relationship between the technology sector and the national government as well as to make strategic investments in research

and technology. The next occupant of the White House must work to align tech companies' missions with collective national interests and policy objectives, improve technological expertise in government, and strengthen the country's ability to exploit its own technological base for national advantage.

By better integrating the tech workforce with the federal government, the United States can build governmental capacity while shrinking the cultural divide. The next administration should pursue a range of programs that lower the barriers to military and public service for citizens with high-tech expertise. The national security community and especially the military can create new on-ramps for established and aspiring tech talent; cultivating a cadre of specialists could then enhance the military's technical competency in areas as diverse as tech procurement and integration, cyber operations and defenses, and intelligence analysis. Beyond the military, new fellowship programs and expansion of existing initiatives can embed recent STEM graduates and more senior tech experts in short-term, high-impact positions in government.[2]

Talent alone cannot bridge the Washington-tech gulf: a new administration must also make strategic investments in the technologies of the future. By increasing government research and development funding and giving additional targeted support to cutting-edge research universities, the next administration can ensure that the country remains at the forefront of innovation, while spurring growth and creating new jobs. It should begin by increasing federal R&D funding to at least its historical average of 1.1 percent of GDP, or $236.94 billion in 2019 dollars. This could be coupled with an additional strategic investment of $100 billion over five years from federal and state governments to support critical technology research at universities in such priority areas as AI, machine learning, data science, quantum computing, personalized medicine, and clean energy. Resources on this scale could boost technological progress by making a market for high-risk, high-reward basic research; founding centers of excellence;

and underwriting loan guarantees that increase the affordability of telecom purchases from U.S. or partner-nation suppliers. A major investment surge should also include significant new funding for scholarships and fellowships, facilities for product fabrication and testing, and seed capital for start-ups.[3]

The next administration must also improve the processes by which the federal government integrates new technologies. Nowhere is this more urgent than in the Department of Defense (DoD). Even as it relies more on commercial technologies, the DoD has inflexible capital allocation and acquisition processes that are at odds with the iterative, agile, and incremental process of private-sector technological development. Though the department is now adapting to deal with start-ups—through such successful pilot programs as In-Q-Tel, DARPA Cyber Fast Track, and DIU—arduous and bureaucratized contracting and procurement procedures continue to dampen collaboration. To accelerate technology adoption, the United States needs a reformed budgeting and contracting process that allows federal agencies greater flexibility to work with start-ups and other small, innovative firms. In addition to encouraging tech adoption, these changes could help the DoD and other agencies do more with existing or limited resources.[4]

This suite of initiatives must be integrated at the highest level of government. The next administration should consider elevating the Office of Science and Technology Policy to a National Emerging Technology Council (NETC) on par with the National Security Council and National Economic Council. A fully staffed and empowered NETC could, for example, oversee the creation of a White House–led interagency national science, technology, and innovation strategy—a plan that could be released in parallel with the National Security Strategy and guide subsequent agency priorities and budget requests. An NETC could also stand up a National Emerging Technology Advisory Board, convening the leaders of America's most strategically consequential technology companies for policy coordination. Cooperation on this scale will reap significant dividends in advancing the United States' technological competitiveness.[5]

In parallel, the United States must also prepare to better defend against malicious cyber activity that threatens global openness. To some extent, this challenge can be addressed through more vigorous regulation. For example, the United States has the ability to impose sanctions on companies that knowingly receive stolen intellectual property—an authority that remains unused.[6] But comprehensive deterrence and defense will be impossible to achieve without ongoing routinized cooperation with the private sector, as companies like banks, defense contractors, and healthcare providers are rich cyber targets, just as social media companies like Facebook and Twitter are major vectors of disinformation. Public-private fusion cells could facilitate continuous monitoring, information sharing, the provision of temporary or specialized security clearances for tech company workers, and rapid response. While these coordination mechanisms can begin as partnerships between the U.S. government and American technology companies, they may evolve to become more inclusive—for example, by establishing mechanisms that allow for ongoing coordination across NATO nations or bilaterally with other treaty allies.[7] Tech companies' internal data can also provide strategic warning and, unlike classified intelligence streams, are more easily shared with partner governments, civil society, and businesses.

In pursuing its objectives, the next administration must embrace the fact that the United States' approach will not resemble China's. Beijing's reliance on state-owned enterprises and national champions, exemplified by the Made in China 2025 plan, reflects a model of state-society relations that America should not replicate. The task for the United States is to harness its tremendous national assets for common purposes: maintaining the technological edge, global market share, and influence over technology standard setting necessary to compete with China and preserve an open international system. Despite obvious differences, the tech sector has an overriding interest in collaborating with Washington in service of openness. If the United States fails to keep its edge and China dominates, U.S. companies may lose access to those markets subsumed within Beijing's bloc; short of this, unwillingness to collaborate may subject them to disadvantageous and potentially odious national regulations. Even from a profit-seeking perspective, therefore, tech companies cannot be agnostic in a global technological competition, particularly one that represents a choice between openness and closure.

Insulating Foreign Policy from Partisan Polarization

Political polarization is enmeshed with a host of other domestic trends and eludes neat policy solutions. Untangling this ghastly web will be a long and tortuous process—in part because polarization undermines the very unity required for bold policy changes. Even when shocking international events, like the terrorist attacks on September 11, 2001, knit the nation together, such unity is transitory and rests fundamentally on favorable economic conditions at home.[8]

For the immediate purposes of American strategy, the next administration must take steps to insulate its foreign policy from partisan political tempests. An openness strategy constitutes a strong foundation for bipartisan cooperation, as many of its pillars enjoy broad-based support from elites of both parties. Democrats and Republicans generally agree that hierarchical dominance of Asia by China or Europe by Russia would adversely affect the United States; they share an interest in continued access to the global commons of sea and space, for both military and commercial purposes; and norms of political independence and democracy support retain currency among foreign policy specialists of both parties. Even as disagreement will likely emerge over the means by which to pursue these ends, these areas of convergence are important nonetheless.

Additionally, Trump's departure from the White House may quickly remove an obstacle to foreign policy consensus on discrete issues. While most lawmakers see Russia as a threat, for example, Republicans have hesitated to back measures that would crack down on election interference lest they be seen as antagonizing the president. Moreover, GOP legislators generally do not approve of Trump's affection for dictators, but are inclined to keep mum for similar reasons. While foreign policy remains polarized, then, broader comity may nonetheless be more possible than is currently apparent.

The next administration must strategically leverage areas of enduring consensus. This will require sustained outreach to Capitol Hill to identify friendly legislators of both parties who can advocate for an openness strategy and ensure it survives partisan tumult. Engagement can begin during the transition period, the seventy-eight days between election and inauguration when administrations begin to articulate their foreign policy priorities via high-level appointments and early communication with legislators. After inauguration, the next administration's first budget and National Security Strategy processes provide opportunities for proactive outreach to Congress and outside experts affiliated with both parties. The next administration can also work with Congress to establish a bipartisan strategy commission and advisory board to review the assumptions and threat assessments that undergird an openness strategy. The commission could follow the model of the National Defense Strategy (NDS) Commission, which convened prominent Democrats and Republicans to assess the feasibility of the Trump administration's NDS, but the body should assemble before strategy documents are drafted and finalized. The administration should also create a bipartisan twenty-first-century Strategy Advisory Board composed of prominent national security figures from both parties to advise on long-term strategy from a cross-cutting, interagency perspective—a task that reaches beyond the scope of extant departmentally specific advisory boards like the Defense Policy Board.

Well beyond the Beltway, the next administration can craft policy initiatives that create enduring alignments between the private sector and openness objectives, thereby protecting core components of the strategy from partisan erraticism. In the tech space, aforementioned initiatives will alter companies' incentives using persuasive as well as coercive tools: for example, major upfront investments in R&D, regulatory or legislative changes that induce deeper cyber security cooperation, and strategic messaging that aims to convince consumers and workforces of the value of pursuing techno-openness in concert with the U.S. government, even when it entails sacrificing short term profit opportunities. The next administration should also seek buy-in from nontech sectors using a blend of carrots and sticks. Particularly because transparent economic development is a central feature of an open international system, active participation by American financial services, energy, and infrastructure firms can propagate investment in critical regions and sectors. Where these industries' incentives are authentically aligned with openness objectives, the strategy will become self-sustaining regardless of who controls the White House—a salutary phenomenon demonstrated by many corporations' commitment to upholding the Paris climate agreement despite the Trump administration's decision to renege, even though they are not formally parties to the accord.

The history of the twentieth century bears important lessons for how polarization might abate over the longer term. There is strong evidence of a "Cold War consensus" uniting Democrats and Republicans behind the central tenets of containment, particularly during the early decades of U.S.-USSR rivalry. This unity had several sources, including the legacy of national service engendered by World War II, the presence of a clear and present danger in the form of the Soviet Union, and declining levels of economic inequality. Re-creating these conditions is not possible or desirable, but policymakers can nonetheless learn from them as they strive for greater consensus. First, they may take novel approaches to civic participation, creating expanded opportunities for military, national, and public service while also enhancing civic education for all young Americans. Second, they should seek to define a common narrative purpose around which Americans can coalesce. While many foreign policy leaders in Washington believe the threat of rising authoritarianism will galvanize the American public, polling suggests that citizens are not particularly energized by looming fears of China and Russia.[9] Instead, it may be the danger, as well as the opportunity, presented by climate change that encourages collective action for common ends, or the call to action for the United States to remain a global leader through innovation and domestic investment. Finally, a central economic priority of the next administration must be mitigation of the economic inequality that plagues the United States and exacerbates polarization.

Preparing for International Competition

As it faces significant domestic pitfalls, American foreign policy is also underequipped for the international environment it will meet—modern competition with great-power rivals. China's ascent gives the United States an economic, technological, and military peer in Asia, rendering the post–Cold War standard of global primacy untenable. But the United States must also prepare for nonmilitary competition that defies the purview of any one agency. Occurring in the space between war and peace, gray zone tactics confound or gradually weaken an adversary's position or resolve without provoking a military response. Precisely because these infractions occur below conventional deterrence thresholds, they present an insidious threat to openness—and one that the United States and its allies are not yet poised to combat. In some cases, Washington can work with its allies and partners to redefine deterrent thresholds to encompass new domains. In other cases, sub-conventional conflict will require new approaches, capabilities, and coordination mechanisms. Openness, therefore, demands an American national security bureaucracy that is equipped to confront a highly variegated and relentlessly dynamic set of challenges.

Revitalizing the State Department

The State Department has an essential role to play in an openness strategy that demands agile multipolar diplomacy with small and middle powers alongside competitive as well as cooperative engagement with great-power rivals. Equipping the department to meet these challenges will require significant capacity-building investments and workforce reforms by the next administration. Resource requirements are all the more acute because the next secretary of state will inherit an infirm department hobbled by Trump administration budget cuts and personnel practices. The next administration must reverse Trump budget cuts, especially in the areas of bilateral economic assistance, international institutions, the global environment, and the Western Hemisphere—all of which are required to sustain an openness strategy. It must also continue higher levels of funding for the Indo-Pacific region, sustain attention on North Korea's nuclear weapons and missiles, and buttress efforts to counter Russian influence in Europe and Eurasia via cyber security, anti-corruption, and support for economic reforms. Although diplomats are ideally suited for preventing and responding to gray zone threats through strategic messaging, the civilian foreign affairs structure stymies action, and the next administration must combat procedural inertia. In tandem, a new administration must expand the Foreign Service with an eye to core diplomatic functions, and should consider a "GI bill for diplomacy" or diplomatic ROTC to help attract top young talent from American universities.[10]

Achieving Military Sufficiency

In the conventional and nuclear domains, the United States must invest in the capabilities required for robust high-end deterrence, understanding that success entails preserving American interests without resorting to war. The military requirements of openness will be most intense in Asia—the region where Chinese ascendance has already ended American global military primacy. The United States and its allies must retain sufficient strength to deter China from making a bid that could result in its hierarchical dominance of any part of the region, to defend against it if it were to mount one, and to keep the global commons open. This will require a First Island Chain defense strategy to counter Chinese anti-access/area-denial (A2/AD) capabilities with land- and sea-based missiles—even though such an ally- and partner-reliant approach will be politically taxing.[11]

In Europe, NATO allies can hold the front lines of regional openness with American support. The United States' nuclear arsenal will remain a cornerstone of deterrence against Russian aggression; at the conventional level, to help deter and defend in high-end conflict, the United States should emphasize NATO partner contributions and training to improve allied readiness and overcome the time-distance problem in the Baltics. Faced with more acute competition in Asia and Europe, the United States should diminish its presence in the Middle East, maintaining only those capabilities required to contain and defeat imminent attacks on the U.S. homeland or troops overseas by state or nonstate actors. American intelligence assets can substitute for a large military footprint in the region by providing "early warning" of emerging threats that could endanger the United States or its overseas interests.[12]

As a general matter, these mission sets will entail prioritizing modernization over the size of end-strength forces, shifting capabilities for large ground operations to national guard and reserve troops, and moving to a tiered readiness model across the services.

Investments should focus on unmanned air and sea systems, space and cyber capabilities, science and technology investments, and special operations forces at the expense of ground forces, manned fighter/attack aircraft, and large surface combatants. To fund requisite force modernization, the next administration must identify opportunities to conserve defense dollars through cuts to the civilian workforce, updates to the military healthcare system, and a rigorous budget survey by the service chiefs and Office of the Secretary of Defense to follow up on the Pentagon's failure of its first-ever audit.[13]

Coordination against Nonmilitary Coercion

In countering gray zone coercion abroad, the United States can draw on its formidable suite of military, economic, diplomatic, and intelligence capabilities to deter or meet such threats forcefully and proportionately. American policy has often struggled to identify creative, calibrated forms of horizontal escalation, whereby the United States and its partners can hold an adversary's interests at risk. Washington possesses a suite of nonmilitary tools for such reprisals, including economic sanctions and trade levers such as pressure via the World Trade Organization; diplomatic steps like curtailment of senior leader engagements or coordination of multilateral condemnations; strategic communications, such as public disclosure of illicit gray zone activities; and legal measures, such as support for dispute settlement through international tribunals. Where the United States seeks to respond with its military, it is advised to produce deterrence by denial as opposed to punishment, sending the message that it will thwart its adversary's ability to accomplish its goals. It can do so by rapidly repositioning forces or deploying strong forward defenses proximate to the initial act of aggression. Not all gray zone challenges are equal, however, and a new administration must assess what sorts of sub-conventional incursions may present real threats to openness, warranting a response—a determination that is likely to vary by region. At the outset of a new administration, the president should issue a directive outlining these elements of a country-specific strategy to counter gray zone coercion and direct supporting departmental action.[14]

Rivals do not only use coercion abroad, however; they have increasingly demonstrated their ability to wield it against the United States at home, weaponizing American domestic openness for adversarial gain. The United States does not presently possess a rubric for diagnosing or responding to foreign interference.[15] An openness strategy points the way to a new framework for engaging cyber incursions, disinformation, and other onslaughts. The strategy's emphasis on political independence enables the national security bureaucracy to identify incursions that aim to subvert elections or other democratic processes; respond by publicizing infractions, thereby reducing their power; and coordinate appropriate reprisals.

Protecting American interests from nonmilitary challenges will require the next administration to rethink the very structure of the national security bureaucracy. Nonmilitary coercion often occurs at interagency "seams," making it all the more difficult to address. The United States can integrate its sub-conventional strategy via the National Security Council at the White House, where a senior director oversees each geographic region and convenes the Defense, State, Treasury, and Commerce Departments as well as the intelligence community (IC). When the threats are domestic, the Departments of Homeland Security and Justice should be involved as well. If this process is embedded within regional directorates at the NSC, nonmilitary challenges will be treated as complex interactions with adversarial nations that warrant interagency responses.[16]

The Changing Nature of Intelligence

Intelligence has a particularly important role to play in this increasingly integrated policy process, and improving analysis of gray zone threats should be a central element of the IC's broader pivot from counterterrorism to great-power competition. As national security threats come from outside the traditional defense domain, options for monitoring them also change. Through private-sector collaboration and the fuller exploitation of commercial tools, the intelligence community can improve its ability to detect military and nonmilitary threats. Commercial sources of geospatial intelligence as well as private-sector monitoring of cyber threats can, for example, significantly expand the underlying database of open source inputs for assessment; AI applications also have the potential to improve gray zone warning by sharpening big-data analysis that detects patterns of malign activity. Such partnerships may create cost efficiencies and improve threat identification while diminishing response time.[17]

Heavier reliance on private-sector tools and collaboration has a significant geopolitical upside: commercially available data are not classified, and can therefore be shared with a much wider range of international partners. Countries with which the United States does not have a close intelligence-sharing arrangement may nonetheless be partners on discrete security challenges—for example, Vietnam with respect to China's militarization of the South China Sea. Public-private intelligence partnerships can generate data that are sharable with state and nonstate partners alike, facilitating the quick and transparent problem identification and attribution necessary to respond to nonmilitary coercion.

Private-Public Openness Abroad

Beyond its traditional tools of foreign policy, the United States has an interest in promoting open norms for commercial interactions among states—whether bilateral or via dedicated institutions. Particularly as China expands its global investment footprint, the United States need not match it symmetrically to prevent Beijing from creating closed spheres of influence. The next administration should work with private-sector partners—domestically and in like-minded nations—to provide selective alternatives to Chinese infrastructure investments around the world. Washington cannot and should not seek to arrest Chinese investment everywhere, but should analyze which types of infrastructure could result in closed spheres—for example, digital infrastructure—and which regions are most vital—for example, the Western Hemisphere—then act accordingly. In essential areas, the United States should use its Overseas Private Investment Corporation and U.S. Export-Import Bank to forge international public-private coalitions.[18]

In those areas deemed nonessential, and where China has already won contracts, Washington can help to monitor Chinese investment for transparency, sustainability, resiliency, and fiscal and social responsibility. By developing and publicizing metrics for policy areas like anti-corruption, digital governance, and extractive industries, U.S.-led initiatives should monitor, promote accountability, and create a basis for American assistance to nations that partner with less than transparent development institutions. If asked, the United States and its partners can offer technical assistance; they can also work with Chinese financial institutions like the Asia Infrastructure Investment Bank to cooperatively promote these standards. The long-term goal of these alternatives should be market diversity: even if this public-private coalition is limited in its scope, recipient nations should have a choice among infrastructure development options, so that Chinese standards do not prevail by default and become a new closed development model.[19]

Alliances and Partnerships

Global alliances and partnerships are integral to the success of an openness strategy, and the next administration must make vigorous, early overtures to repair these damaged relationships. Advanced economies with significant technological market share, the United States and its allies possess more than 28 times China's overall GDP and exceed its per capita wealth by a multiple of 4.5; if allied nations share the United States' commitment to openness, this coalition can ensure that large swaths of Europe and Asia, as well as significant portions of the global economy, remain free and accessible.[20] Allies can also join with Washington in advancing openness in new regions and domains, leveraging their highly capable economies, militaries, and tech sectors. Moreover, strong alliance ties will make it easier to weather inevitable disagreements that emerge due to conflicting national interests. As twenty-first-century geopolitics become increasingly multipolar, especially in the Indo-Pacific, strong alliances will help the United States ensure that pivotal middle powers are on the side of openness.

The United States must do more than simply recommit to its alliances, however; the next administration must also pursue a modernization agenda. America's alliances boast an astounding record of success over their seventy-year history. Yet an openness strategy will require Washington to expand its treaty alliances in directions their architects could not have imagined. Particularly as international order becomes more hotly contested and power shifts toward China, close political, economic, technological, and security coordination with allies will be essential if the United States is to promote openness. Allies are becoming all the more necessary even as they are experiencing economic and demographic stagnation themselves, and Washington will need to craft sustainable new alliance strategies to accomplish its goals.[21]

The United States and its allies must move beyond their traditional focus on deterrence and defense in high-end conflict, as well as their more recent engagement in low-intensity peacekeeping or counterinsurgency operations. Efforts to counter nonmilitary coercion will vary by alliance, yet each U.S. ally will face a range of sub-conventional challenges. A central task for each alliance will be to distinguish what action those challenges require: deterrence, punitive responses, or no reprisals at all. NATO, for example, presently lacks robust cyber information-sharing mechanisms—the development of which could significantly enhance defenses via improved situational awareness and, in turn, facilitate collective defense, if that ever became necessary.[22]

The United States should also integrate its efforts to propound global openness in concert with its allies. In maintaining open commons in the sea and space, allies are natural partners. Allies should form the core of freedom-of-navigation (FON) coalitions in Africa and the Middle East and of FON-related information sharing in Asia. They may help to coordinate international legal advocacy, sanctions for egregious violations of international law, and "naming and shaming" efforts to publicize malign behavior that jeopardizes global commons.

Allied nations are the front line for the United States' policy of democracy support, and Washington should take a stronger approach to democratic backsliding among alliance members. Currently, NATO has no clear procedure for monitoring democratic degradation in member states, nor does it have a probationary status that could allow the alliance to audit serious backsliding. Although difficult to implement, such a status could allow alliances to better promote democratic values and processes. While on probation, alliance members could remain covered by Article V but would face scrutiny until their governments could pass a "democratic values check"; possible measures could include exclusion from NATO's Nuclear Planning Group or other highly sensitive bodies, restrictions on officials' eligibility for the most senior positions in the NATO Secretariat or military command structure, and exclusion from military exercises. By insisting upon shared values within its alliances, the United States can ensure that its alliances do not become vectors of closure from within.[23]

Furthermore, allies can advance the principles of openness as the West grapples with the global growth of Chinese power. Particularly in those areas where the United States cannot compete with China on its own—for example, in the development and global rollout of high-speed 5G wireless technologies—allies are an invaluable asset. Indeed, the United States may have a particular opportunity to bring together allies and partners from states like the UK, Germany, Japan, South Korea, Australia, Israel, Finland, and Sweden into a pooled 5G network that competes with China's state-backed 5G leader Huawei via an innovative form of international public-private partnership. Similar collaborative opportunities exist for AI investment as well.[24]

Alongside formal allies, the next administration should cultivate a network of global partners in strategically vital regions. Unlike alliances, these partnerships will be more issue-specific and opportunistic, predicated on mutual interests rather than open-ended treaty commitments. India, for example, may not align with openness principles on every matter of global or regional governance—but when it does, the United States should seize the opportunity to bring Delhi into its coalition.

The United States should also pursue partnerships with middle powers and strategically consequential small states, even if they are not democracies. Such partners—like Vietnam, a nominally Communist single-party state, and politically tumultuous, territorially riven Ukraine—can serve as regional counterweights to China and Russia, and they may support open governance in discrete domains. In many cases, the opening salvos of these approaches should be technology- or investment-based, particularly in Asia, where prospective partners are especially wary of overt security balancing against China, but are clamoring to secure their place on the global supply chain. Additionally, the next administration should carve out a category of relationships that are neither allies nor partners but rather alignments of convenience characterized by quiet and episodic cooperation. Where the United States engages in military cooperation with such states, it should be primarily defensive in nature, with the understanding that U.S. initiatives are likely to exist alongside cooperation with China and may ultimately deteriorate amid intensified pressure from Beijing. Despite a vestigial treaty, for example, Thailand belongs in this category. Such variegated forms of alliance and alignment are an inevitable feature of multi-polarity; U.S. policy should position the United States to capitalize on this dynamism, rather than curtailing prospective partnerships by limiting cooperation to liberal states.

Building International Order for the Twenty-First Century

In pursuing a strategy of openness, the United States must also seek to renovate international order to make it resilient to the major domestic and international shifts under way. Such a strategy should seek to modernize some existing international institutions in collaboration with allies and partners; it should also develop new regimes in undergoverned areas in which Washington has a clear interest in setting norms and rules to prevent closure. Where the United States finds it harder to conclude new legal agreements, it can pursue less formal but nonetheless powerful cooperation. Procedurally, the next administration can learn from the examples of the Iran nuclear deal—an agreement negotiated between the five permanent UNSC members, Germany, and Iran, but ultimately codified in UNSC resolutions and implemented in concert with the International Atomic Energy Agency (IAEA)—as well as the Paris Accord, which forged an international agreement on the basis of 196 national plans. New agreements do not require initial, universal, and uniform buy-in to shape geopolitics.

In a system that includes authoritarian competitors, however, it would be naïve to expect Beijing or Moscow to merely accept an American vision for the future of global order. Order building in the twenty-first century will itself be competitive, as the United States and China forge systems that suit each country's national interests and values. The future order will not, therefore, be universally open, or even universally ordered. As has been true in the past, the nature of order will likely vary in functional scope, geography, and formality. Functionally, future order will be eclectic, with novel, specific forms of governance for emerging domains like technology and climate existing alongside sweeping legacy structures like the UN. Geographically, many elements of global order will remain, but the regional order in Asia will become notably thicker, as the United States and China compete over order and Beijing assumes a larger leadership role, while the United States and Europe retain their regional ordering roles in the West. Future order will also assume diverse forms, as some elements like the trade regime will be highly institutionalized with legal enforcement mechanisms, whereas others will be informally predicated on interest convergence, such as norms to govern cyber activities or voluntary space launch notifications.

Given this diversity, no single state or institution will assume universal ordering authority. For this precise reason, in some areas—most notably in the realm of internet governance and possibly trade—Washington may need to focus its attention on solidifying coalitions of like-minded partners and preventing antithetical norms from dominating. Under more propitious circumstances, small yet mighty coalitions can shape other states' incentives and create pressure toward the creation of new universal rules, whether embedded in legacy institutions, enshrined in new ones, or enacted through informal means. Finally, and despite their divergent order preferences, the United States and China will still find it necessary to create new ordering arrangements for transnational challenges.

Maintaining Open Global Commons

The United States has a vital national interest in preserving the openness of the global commons of sea, air, and space. The most obvious challenges to maritime openness are in Asia and the Middle East. In Asia, China's growing naval as well as anti-access/area-denial capabilities present Beijing with the option of coercively limiting freedom of navigation within the First Island Chain during wartime, increasing its coercive power in peacetime; it asserts the primacy of its domestic laws over the UN Convention on the Law of the Sea with no legal basis, has conducted illegal island reclamation, and has attempted to forestall lawful military passage. Since the early Cold War, Washington has understood the First Island Chain archipelago to be its defensive front line, but China's A2/AD approach makes the direct defense of allies increasingly tenuous. Washington must move toward an integrated counter-A2/AD strategy, while also strengthening its position in Southeast Asia. It should buttress capacity-building efforts with Vietnam, Indonesia, and the Philippines, prioritize defense cooperation with India, and synchronize similar disparate efforts with Japan and Australia. It must also increase significantly its foreign military financing to the region, so that regional states are better positioned to help keep the seas open.[25]

The United States faces no peer competitor in the Middle East and North Africa, but open global commons are not assured. States like Iran as well as pirates or terrorist groups could imperil international waterways even if they cannot close a sphere. The next administration should spearhead multilateral freedom of navigation coalitions in the Horn of Africa and the Straits of Hormuz. Presently, three different multilateral coalitions conduct counter-piracy operations in the region—led by the United States, NATO, and the EU—while numerous other states, including China, Russia, and India, operate independently. Furthermore, given Iranian threats to shipping in the Gulf, the next administration can build on the Trump administration's efforts to generate support from allies and partners for situational awareness, maritime escorts, and assistance to endangered vessels.[26]

The United States will be better positioned to influence outcomes if it finally ratifies UNCLOS, which legally codifies the openness of the maritime commons. The United States led the original UNCLOS negotiations and has signed the treaty, which counts China,

Russia, India, Japan, and Germany as members. Not only is UNC-LOS the body of law that provides a basis for keeping the seas open in the Gulf and the South China Sea, it also applies to newly disputed waters like the Arctic. An early push for ratification by the next administration can capitalize on enduring bipartisan support for UNCLOS.

Space increases in importance as satellite networks have become fundamental to modern communication technology utilized for commerce and national security. Yet the sole governing instrument, the Outer Space Treaty (OST), entered into force more than fifty years ago. Procedurally, it lacks mechanisms for settling disputes and contains major substantive gaps or ambiguities on critical issues like space debris, asset interference, commercialization, and weaponization. The next administration should assume a leadership role in ongoing negotiations in the UN Committee on the Peaceful Uses of Outer Space. Washington can also work with Russia and China on needed reforms, such as on prior notification of space maneuvers and protocols for launch site visits. Although a comprehensive space governance arrangement is unlikely to materialize, clear norms can proscribe unacceptable behavior, reinforce deterrence, and reduce the risk of miscalculation and accidents, and may eventually be formalized in arms control or new legal instruments. Discussion of space norms should be commonplace in bilateral engagement between the United States, Russia, and China, including in areas of clear disagreement.[27]

Modernizing the Trade Regime

The free-trade regime has conferred significant benefits upon the United States, but it has also allowed more closed societies to exploit openness to their advantage—and to the detriment of workers worldwide, including in the United States. To address these shortcomings, the next administration must reform the global trade regime through an interlocking series of steps that allows open states to reap economic benefits without exploitation. This process may begin with WTO reform, but trade renewal will need to proceed through three reinforcing approaches: realistically resetting the rules of international trade by modernizing the WTO, affirmatively shaping the global economic environment through high-standards multilateral free-trade agreements, and protecting sensitive technologies and industries that may otherwise be exploited. In many of these efforts, the primary antagonist to trade openness is China—though the United States cannot craft its trade policy on the basis of geopolitics alone. Washington must calibrate the speed, substance, and sequencing of its foreign economic policy agenda with a view toward its domestic economic and political effects. While the following steps will not rectify many of trade's distributional consequences within the United States, they represent the international pillar of a trade strategy that must proceed in tandem with domestic policy reforms that address trade-related inequality and job loss directly.

Reforming a sclerotic WTO is an arduous and complex undertaking, but one the next administration must attempt. A failure to do so will mean that nonmarket economies continue to capitalize on trade openness to advance their own closed systems. Washington should commence with an early push to reform the process for resolving trade disputes; it must also attempt to rewrite WTO rules to crack down on prejudicial government subsidies to state-owned enterprises, the lack of which has allowed China and other nonmarket economies to take advantage of international market openness; and it must modernize WTO rules for new domains. In the immediate term, the WTO faces serious legislative and adjudicative atrophy, for which the United States bears substantial responsibility. No WTO reform agenda can proceed until member states break their impasse over appointments of new appellate judges for dispute settlement, particularly on trade remedy cases. A package of procedural reforms that streamlines the appeals process while limiting its scope for interpreting domestic law is a prerequisite if the United States and like-minded partners are to advance a broader reform agenda of far-reaching significance.[28]

An open economic order will also require Washington to push for WTO reform on state subsidies—areas in which major economies, including China and India, present significant challenges—with a particular focus on the market-distorting effects of state-owned enterprises (SOEs). They and many others slip through existing WTO rules to use state subsidies as nontariff barriers—a practice that now affects nearly 70 percent of world trade. The next administration should lead the development of a code of SOE conduct that draws upon underutilized state subsidy rules within the WTO framework, including clauses in the original GATT charter and other agreements. By integrating rules to which members have already agreed, rather than creating new ones, the United States can use a code of conduct to signal its unwillingness to abide prejudicial behavior, help draw legal bright lines, and build a coalition of like-minded states behind its preferred SOE standards. A code could also create new rules for transparency and subsidy notifications by member states, with verification measures and stricter punishments for noncompliance. This effort can then serve as the basis for new cases that Washington can bring against SOE violators, most notably China—which tends to comply with WTO rulings.[29]

Modernizing the WTO will also entail updating its rules for the age of digital commerce, particularly on cross-border data flows, localization laws, and national treatment of product and service exporters. The next administration should reinvigorate negotiations over a Trade in Services Agreement (TiSA), which seeks to expand market access beyond current commitments, increase transparency, set common rules for digital trade, and ensure fair competition with SOEs. These rules will almost certainly begin as an agreement among a subset of WTO members, and while it may initially exclude major exporters like China and India, it could nevertheless represent

70 percent of world trade in services. TiSA may thus exemplify a useful outside-in approach to WTO reform, whereby economically significant blocs of states agree to new rules that come to shape the behavior of other major trading partners. Renewed American trade initiatives for Asia would have similarly salutary effects, as discussed below. By restoring appellate functionality, cracking down on SOEs, and updating rules for the digital economy, a U.S.-led WTO reform effort can help to ensure that the body remains the fulcrum of an open trading regime, rather than abetting practices that advantage shuttered systems.[30]

Some of these reforms may prove nearly impossible to enact within the consensus-based WTO, but by leading the charge, the United States can create a coalition of member states that agree to function by higher and more open standards, preserving and extending rules even if only a subset of members abide by them.[31] In tandem with WTO modernization efforts, therefore, the next administration can reshape the geoeconomic landscape by helping to lead a multilateral open trade regime. Such a strategy could seek to integrate environmental and climate priorities, labor protections, and intellectual property rights with unencumbered flows of goods and services, thereby providing economic benefits to both source and destination countries. Though falling short of the WTO's near-universal scope of inclusion, these agreements would be more readily achievable and would restructure the incentives nonparticipant countries like China face, improving the prospects for an accessible trading order.[32]

Perhaps the multilateral step that would make the highest impact would be to rejoin the Trans-Pacific Partnership (formerly TPP, now known as CPTPP). Some of Washington's biggest issues with Chinese trade practices, including technology transfers and intellectual property violations, are not subject to WTO rules. Many of these receive explicit coverage in the revived version of TPP, which counts eleven Pacific Rim nations as signatories, and includes advanced economies as well as developing nations, giving it a diverse imprimatur as the next era of trade standards. A U.S. return would create an enormous free-trade zone, which would incentivize China to improve its own practices. Subsequently, the WTO could adopt CPTPP rules that reflect the massive changes in trade and investment patterns since the mid-1990s. The CPTPP is not a perfect agreement—it does not explicitly cover currency manipulation, for example—but the United States could insist upon favorable modifications to issues like intellectual property protections as a condition for reentry. If rejoining the CPTPP remains politically infeasible, however, a new administration could consider reverse-engineering the outcome through a series of bilateral or plurilateral pacts. Such an effort would be more onerous, but could deflect some of the political ire associated with the TPP. The next administration should also explore new high-standards agreements with the EU and Britain in an effort to identify deal parameters that would satisfy domestic constituencies on both sides of the Atlantic.[33]

Where a two-tiered approach fails to address critical economic or national security concerns, the United States may resort to unilateral but surgical fixes. An open economic order will require the United States to eschew the idea of widespread economic decoupling from China: the two economies are much too entangled to make such a schism feasible, and the virtues of interdependence render it undesirable as well. Nevertheless, targeted trade remedies like anti-dumping measures may be necessary to prevent China from exploiting American economic openness for unfair gain. Amid heightened geostrategic competition, the U.S. government will also need to consider increasing its protection of highly sensitive industries and technologies from China, imposing calibrated restrictions on trade in national security–relevant technologies and applying closer scrutiny of Chinese investments with potential geopolitical significance. The objective of this strategy should be to lead huge portions of the global economy toward high-standards trade openness, protecting only those industries and technologies that might otherwise be abused by the forces of closure. To the extent that China refuses to change its ways, an openness strategy equips the United States to offset the worst effects of prejudicial economic practices and preserve its national security while continuing to harvest the benefits of economic exchange.

Internet Governance, AI, and Cyber Security

In areas of rapid technological change, such as internet governance, cyber, and AI, vigorous interstate competition has begun, yet no clear rules exist. With China and Russia preferring alternative governance models, the United States must set rules and norms with like-minded countries to prevent authoritarian competitors from setting their own. Washington must cooperate with partner states, tech sectors, and civil societies to advance a multi-stakeholder coalition to address issues of data storage, privacy, and cyber crime and hacking. Autocratic preferences for closed internets may lead to internet balkanization or "splinternets"—but the United States should lead the charge toward an open and pluralistic information environment that encourages democracy, benefits it economically, and protects the American system from the most pernicious forms of foreign attacks. Where interests converge with China and Russia, the next administration should also advance common interpretations of international law and pursue joint technological "rules of the road" via the UN or other fora; so too should Washington explore opportunities to expand the norms of technological openness to include authoritarian and mixed regimes.[34]

Similar principles apply to other domains of technological innovation, like AI and cyber. The United States can achieve two forms of ordering in this regard: establish new deterrence thresholds in competitive spaces where none exist, and create new national security norms and rules. By clarifying how cyber thresholds may trigger alliance mutual-defense commitments, the United States can improve deterrence in cyberspace. It could, for example, craft a declaratory policy that identifies the types of cyber activities that may fall under the UN definition of a "use of force," while preserving flexibility on the form that response would take.

In building new norms and rules, Washington can collaborate with coalitions of partners and take better advantage of regimes that already exist. By virtue of its long-standing innovation edge, the United States has implicitly set global standards on emerging technologies, but has limited its involvement with international bodies fit for this task. As China has emerged as a peer technological competitor, Beijing has begun to set specifications for 5G and AI, among other technologies, increasing the chances that it will dominate these fields. Working with like-minded countries, companies, and organizations, Washington must lead efforts to set standards in new technical domains, ensuring that the venues as well as the rules themselves advance an open technology landscape. Washington can also collaborate with like-minded countries to draft preliminary codes of conduct for cyber and AI, focusing on tough issues like cyber attacks on critical infrastructure. It should support codes developed by close allies, particularly where they are faithful to the American preference for multi-stakeholder governance and open information environments. Such codes could, at best, serve as the basis for future arms control negotiations—even if they take on the informal character of the 2015 U.S.-China cyber agreement—and at worst, they would make it more difficult for antithetical norms to coalesce unopposed.[35]

Climate, Migration, and Global Health

The United States and its partners can support new forms of cooperation on migration, climate change, and global pandemics, as all three represent shared challenges with the potential to massively disrupt economies and polities around the globe. Climate change is likely to result in over 100 million displaced persons in Africa, Southeast Asia, and Latin America, and the United States and allied countries will remain obvious havens for climate refugees. Rather than wait for disasters to spur migration crises, Washington and its partners should begin to craft a more systematic migration regime now. By definition, such an effort cannot promote completely open borders in Europe, Asia, and the United States, but rather must seek to manage migration consistently and transparently.[36]

Moreover, the looming threats of climate change and global pandemics demand further order building. The United States should rejoin the Paris Climate Agreement and expand its scope by lobbying other major emitters to ramp up the ambition of their domestic climate targets, work to ensure commitments are transparent and enforceable, and stem cheating through punitive trade measures. To exceed its own Paris targets and set aggressive new ones, the United States will have to embrace more regulation on activities ranging from greenhouse gas emissions to energy efficiency, while also investing seriously in the R&D, job training, and infrastructure upgrades required to transition toward a green economy.[37] Governance regimes for global health, including pandemics, are sparse.

Further, as the United States seeks to keep Asia open amid China's rise, climate and health-related projects should be part of a mixed cooperative-competitive strategy. American BRI alternatives should include a focus on climate change resilience planning. Relying on private-public cooperation and conducted with high environmental standards, these projects present obvious opportunities to work with allies; they may also allow for collaboration with Beijing. As one of the major powers that will lead the future climate and health regimes, China has an incentive to contribute to these efforts, and Washington can encourage it to raise its environmental and governance standards, at least on shared projects. Climate, migration, and global health present grievous social, political, and economic threats that are unlikely to abate: if they hold a salutary flicker, it is in their potential to galvanize new forms of cooperation, even among competitors. The United States must therefore commit itself to competitive order building lest closed alternatives exclude its interests, while remaining open to new forms of cooperation.

UN Security Council Reform

As these transnational challenges vividly illustrate, a central feature of an open international system must be cooperation among great powers on issues of mutual interest. For all that they seek revisions to many aspects of international order, Beijing and Moscow ardently support the UN as a cornerstone. Given the alignment between the core principles of the UN Charter and the animating tenets of openness, this support is a source of leverage for the United States. In the years to come, the UNSC could face a mounting legitimacy crisis, as its representation decreasingly reflects global power distributions. Given German, Japanese, and Indian support for Security Council reform to broaden the membership, the next administration should advocate for reforms that incorporate emerging powers that are democratic, share a commitment to global openness, make major contributions to peace and security, and support the UN budget.[38]

Because of their growing economic and geopolitical power, India, Germany, and Japan stand out as top candidates for UNSC inclusion. The United States could propose a provisional status for new permanent members whereby their veto power would be suspended for the first fifteen years—as India has itself suggested—then subject to review and final approval by the original Permanent Five members. This change could be part of a broader reform package that also adds four nonpermanent but reelectable seats, distributed evenly across Africa, Asia, Latin America and the Caribbean, and Eastern Europe.[39] Even if reform efforts ultimately founder—and opposition by China and Russia to expansion does not bode well—the United States can use its advocacy as an opportunity to demonstrate the benefits of participation in an American-led open, inclusive international system, drawing a comparison to the visions of international order proffered by great-power competitors. Additionally, this push may help to win Delhi's cooperation in other order-building areas, such as internet governance.

The Day After Trump

The temptation to avoid hard choices is undeniable. Domestic divisions obscure and obstruct the coalescence of a new foreign policy consensus, making quixotic bids for restoration of traditional frameworks the path of least resistance for leaders of both political parties. By returning to proven international affairs shibboleths rather than attempting a vast, novel agenda under conditions of constraint, policymakers may understandably rationalize, the United States can work incrementally but diligently to restore its standing in the world. Such illusions reflect sins not of intention but of omission: restorationists have failed to calculate that the trends underlying many of the Trump presidency's tribulations will not abate when he departs the Oval Office.

The day after Trump is nothing less than an extraordinary moment of opportunity. As with post–natural disaster recovery, American foreign policy can "build back better" if, when the chaos breaks, it reassesses its surroundings, audits its capabilities, and adapts its global aims. This era-defining moment is simply too momentous to pass up—for, with the passage of time, malleability will give way to resistance and advantages will attenuate. If the United States fails to seize the initiative, its power to order international politics will wane, magnifying the prospect that global closure will menace American prosperity and security in ways unseen in the postwar era.

The pursuit of an openness strategy and the policy pillars to support it is undeniably a vast undertaking. It requires a recalibration of the United States' role in the world not seen since the mid- to late 1940s, when Washington urgently tied its foreign policy fate to international order; it calls for cooperation between the public and private sectors and among allies on a scale that is just as uncommon. Protecting and exploiting American domestic strength amid tumult, reorganizing foreign policy for competition despite overwhelming inertia, and modernizing proven institutions while building urgently needed new ones is a mandate so vast that no one administration could hope to achieve it. Surely, parts of the pursuit will fail. A splinternet may emerge, the trading regime will remain imperfect, and nonmilitary coercion will overcome attempts to deter it, all despite Washington's best efforts to pursue global openness. Yet even if some initiatives founder, partial success will preserve openness in significant domains and regions, with American vital interests significantly more secure than if Washington succumbed to apathy and inaction.

With a clear strategic vision and the policies to support it, the next administration can bring unifying purpose to American foreign policy. Indeed, the agenda we lay out is no bigger than the charge it seeks to address—the chance to reconceive America's role in the world and the organization of the international system in the face of historic global change, such that each continues to redound to America's overwhelming interests. If the United States fails to assume this mantle of leadership, it will find itself utterly ill equipped for the world it will face in ten years' time—a world increasingly disordered, or perhaps ordered according to antithetical norms, and in which its dearest economic, political, and security objectives are far from guaranteed. If it seizes this opportunity, however, Washington can preside over an open world that will keep it safe and prosperous for decades to come. In this mandate, there can be no delay; the day after will not come again.

Notes

ONE

Power, Strategy, and Order

1. Kori Schake, "The Trump Doctrine Is Winning and the World Is Losing," *New York Times*, June 15, 2018, https://www.nytimes.com/2018/06/15/opinion/sunday/trump-china-america-first.html; Robert Kagan, "Welcome to the Jungle," *Washington Post*, October 9, 2018, https://www.washingtonpost.com/opinions/welcome-to-the-jungle/2018/10/09/0f8ffb58-cbc5–11e8-a3e6–44daa3d35ede_story.html?utm_term=.9231deb867f4; Thomas Wright, "The Foreign Crises Awaiting Trump," *Atlantic*, January 20, 2017, https://www.theatlantic.com/international/archive/2017/01/trump-russia-putin-north-korea-putin/513749/; Stewart M. Patrick, "An Open World Is in the Balance. What Might Replace the Liberal Order?" Council on Foreign Relations, January 10, 2017, http://blogs.cfr.org/patrick/2017/01/10/an-open-world-is-in-the-balance-what-might-replace-the-liberal-order/; Jeremi Suri, "How Trump's Executive Orders Could Set America Back 70 Years," *Atlantic*, January 27, 2017, https://www.theatlantic.com/politics/archive/2017/01/trumps-executive-orders-will-set-america-back-70-years/514730/; Richard N. Haass, "Liberal World Order, R.I.P.," Council on Foreign Relations, March 21, 2018, https://www.cfr.org/article/liberal-world-order-rip.

2. Patrick Porter, "A World Imagined: Nostalgia and the Liberal World Order," CATO Institute Policy Analysis, June 5, 2018, https://www.cato.org/publications/policy-analysis/world-imagined-nostalgia-liberal-order; Andrew Bacevich, "The Global Order Myth," *American Conservative*, June 15, 2017,

https://www.theamericanconservative.com/articles/the-global-order-myth/; Naazneen Barma, Ely Ratner, and Steven Weber, "The Mythical Liberal Order," *National Interest*, no. 124 (March/April 2013): 56–67; Nick Danforth, "What's So Disordered about Your World Order?" *War on the Rocks*, June 20, 2018, https://warontherocks.com/2018/06/whats-so-disordered-about-your-world-order/; Paul Staniland, "Misreading the 'Liberal Order': Why We Need New Thinking in American Foreign Policy," *Lawfare*, July 29, 2018, https://www.lawfareblog.com/misreading-liberal-order-why-we-need-new-thinking-american-foreign-policy.

3. G. John Ikenberry, "The End of the Liberal International Order?" *International Affairs* 94, no. 1 (January 2018): 7–23; Constance Duncombe and Tim Dunne, "After Liberal World Order," *International Affairs* 94, no. 1 (January 2018): 25–42; Jahn Beate, "Liberal Internationalism: Historical Trajectory and Current Prospects," *International Affairs* 94, no. 1 (January 2018): 43–61; Daniel Deudney and G. John Ikenberry, "Liberal World: The Resilient Order," *Foreign Affairs* 97, no. 4 (July/August 2018): 16–24; Jeff D. Colgan and Robert O. Keohane, "The Liberal Order Is Rigged: Fix It Now or Watch It Wither," *Foreign Affairs* 96, no. 3 (May/June 2017): 36–44; James M. Goldgeier, "The Misunderstood Roots of the International Order—and Why They Matter Again," *Washington Quarterly* 41, no. 3 (2018): 15; Bruce W. Jentleson, "The Liberal Order Isn't Coming Back: What Next?" *Democracy: A Journal of Ideas*, no. 48 (2018), https://democracyjournal.org/magazine/48/the-liberal-order-isnt-coming-back-what-next/; Heather Hurlburt, "Foreign Policy After Trump: The U.S. Has Homework to Do," *Lawfare*, June 26, 2018, https://www.lawfareblog.com/foreign-policy-after-trump-us-has-homework-do; Rebecca Lissner and Mira Rapp-Hooper, "The Day After Trump: American Strategy for a New International Order," *Washington Quarterly* 41, no. 1 (2018): 7–25.

4. Dan Drezner, "This Time Is Different: Why US Foreign Policy Will Never Recover," *Foreign Affairs* 98, no. 3 (May/June 2019): 10–17; Hurlburt, "Foreign Policy After Trump"; Staniland, "Misreading the 'Liberal Order' "; Bruce Jentleson, "The Post-Liberal International Order World: Some Core Characteristics," *Lawfare*, September 9, 2018, https://www.lawfareblog.com/post-liberal-international-order-world-some-core-characteristics.

5. E.g., Stephen Brooks, G. John Ikenberry, and William Wohlforth, "Don't Come Home, America: The Case against Retrenchment," *International Security* 37, no. 3 (2013): 10; Barry Posen, "A New U.S. Grand Strategy," *Boston Review*, July 1, 2014, http://bostonreview.net/us/barry-r-posen-restraint-grand-strategy-united-states.

6. G. John Ikenberry, *After Victory: Institutions, Strategic Restraint, and the Rebuilding of Order After Major Wars* (Princeton: Princeton University Press, 2000); Hedley Bull, *The Anarchical Society: A Study of Order in World Politics* (London: Palgrave Macmillan, 1977).

7. G. John Ikenberry, "The Logic of Order: Westphalia, Liberalism, and the Evolution of International Order in the Modern Era," in *Power, Order and Change in World Politics*, ed. G. John Ikenberry (Princeton: Princeton University Press, 2014), 87.

8. Gideon Rose, "The Fourth Founding: The United States and the Liberal Order," *Foreign Affairs* 98, no. 1 (January/February 2019): 20.

9. Michael Mazaar, "The Real History of the International Order: Neither Myth nor Accident," *Foreign Affairs*, August 7, 2018, https://www.foreignaffairs.com/articles/2018-08-07/real-history-liberal-order.

10. John Mearsheimer, "Bound to Fail: The Rise and Fall of the Liberal International Order," *International Security* 43, no. 4 (Spring 2019): 7–50.

11. Robert Dahl, "The Concept of Power," *Behavioral Science* 2, no. 3 (Spring 1957): 201–15; William Wohlforth, *The Elusive Balance: Power and Perceptions during the Cold War* (Ithaca: Cornell University Press, 1993), 4.

12. Rebecca Friedman Lissner, "What Is Grand Strategy? Sweeping a Conceptual Minefield," *Texas National Security Review*, November 2018, https://tnsr.org/2018/11/what-is-grand-strategy-sweeping-a-conceptual-minefield/; Graham Allison, "The Myth of the Liberal Order," *Foreign Affairs*, July/August 2018, https://www.foreignaffairs.com/articles/2018-06-14/myth-liberal-order; Staniland, "Misreading the 'Liberal Order.'"

13. Kyle Lascurettes, "Orders of Exclusion: The Strategic Sources of Foundational Rules in International Relations," unpublished MS, June 2018, 17; Ikenberry, "The Logic of Order," 85; Rebecca Lissner and Mira Rapp-Hooper, "The Liberal International Order in Crisis" (paper presented at International Studies Association, Toronto, March 27, 2019), 3, 29–30.

14. Ikenberry, "The Logic of Order," 86; Daniel H. Nexon and Thomas Wright, "What's at Stake in the American Empire Debate," *American Political Science Review* 101, no. 2 (May 2007): 253–71; G. John Ikenberry, "Liberalism and Empire: Logics of Order in the American Unipolar Age," *Review of International Studies* 30, no. 4 (October 2004): 609–30. For a classic take on the rise and fall of empires, see Robert Gilpin, *War and Change in World Politics* (Cambridge: Cambridge University Press, 1981).

15. Kalevi Holsti, *Peace and War: Armed Conflicts and International Order, 1648–1989* (Cambridge: Cambridge University Press, 1990).

16. Richard Haass, *A World in Disarray* (New York: Penguin Books, 2017); Holsti, *Peace and War*, 39; Peter Wilson, *The Thirty Years' War: Europe's Tragedy* (Cambridge, MA: Harvard University Press, 2011), 753–54.

17. Holsti, *Peace and War*, 40.

18. Henry Kissinger, *A World Restored: Europe After Napoleon; The Politics of Conservatism in a Revolutionary Age* (New York: Grosset and Dunlap, 1957), 4.

19. Holsti, *Peace and War*, 125.

20. Haass, *A World in Disarray*, 25.

21. Holsti, *Peace and War*, 131.

22. Haass, *A World in Disarray*, 25–26.
23. David Kang, *East Asia before the West: Five Centuries of Trade and Tribute* (New York: Columbia University Press, 2010), 7, 15.
24. Warren I. Cohen, *East Asia at the Center: Four Thousand Years of Engagement with the World* (New York: Columbia University Press, 2000), 151; Kang, *East Asia before the West*, 55.
25. Zheng Feng, "Rethinking the Tribute System: Broadening the Conceptual Horizon of Historical East Asian Politics," *Chinese Journal of International Politics* 2, no. 4 (Winter 2009): 551; Ji-Young Lee, *China's Hegemony: Four Hundred Years of East Asian Domination* (New York: Columbia University Press, 2016).
26. Kang, *East Asia before the West*, 1, 2, 71; Yuan-Kang Wang, "Explaining the Tribute System: Power, Confucianism, and War in Medieval East Asia," *Journal of East Asian Studies* 13, no. 2 (August 2013): 214.
27. G. John Ikenberry, "Liberal Internationalism 3.0: America and the Dilemmas of Liberal World Order," *Perspective on Politics* 7, no. 1 (March 2009): 71–87; John Bew, "World Order: Many-Headed Monster or Noble Pursuit?" *Texas National Security Review*, November 24, 2017, https://tnsr.org/2017/11/world-order-many-headed-monster-noble-pursuit/.
28. Thomas Knock, *To End All Wars: Woodrow Wilson and the Quest for a New World Order* (New York: Oxford University Press, 1992), 143–44.
29. Holsti, *Peace and War*, 210; Oona Hathaway and Scott Shapiro, *The Internationalists: How a Radical Plan to Outlaw War Remade the World* (New York: Simon and Schuster, 2017).
30. Haass, *A World in Disarray*, 31.
31. Mazaar, "The Real History of the International Order"; G. John Ikenberry, *Liberal Leviathan: The Origins, Crisis, and Transformation of the American World Order* (Princeton: Princeton University Press, 2012), 217; Lascurettes, "Orders of Exclusion," 316; "Third International," *Encyclopedia Britannica*, https://www.britannica.com/topic/Third-International; "Comecon," *Encyclopedia Britannica*, https://www.britannica.com/topic/Comecon.
32. Haass, *A World in Disarray*, 54.
33. Bew, "World Order"; Ikenberry, "Liberal Internationalism 3.0"; Alastair Iain Johnston, "The Failures of the 'Failure of Engagement' with China," *Washington Quarterly* 42, no. 2 (2019): 100–103.
34. Staniland, "Misreading the 'Liberal Order' "; Daniel Sargent, *A Superpower Transformed: The Remaking of American Foreign Relations in the 1970s* (New York: Oxford University Press, 2015); Rebecca Lissner and Mira Rapp-Hooper, "The Liberal Order Is More Than a Myth," *Foreign Affairs*, July 31, 2018, https://www.foreignaffairs.com/articles/world/2018-07-31/liberal-order-more-myth?cid=int-fls&pgtype=hpg.
35. According to Polity IV data: *Polity IV: Regime Authority Characteristics and Transitions Datasets* (2018), distributed by Center for Systemic Peace, https://libguides.webster.edu/data/chicago. Drew Desilver, "Despite Global Con-

cerns about Democracy, More Than Half of Countries Are Democratic," Pew Research Center, May 14, 2019, https://www.pewresearch.org/fact-tank/2019 /05/14/more-than-half-of-countries-are-democratic/.

36. Max Roser, "Democracy," Our World in Data, June 2019, https://ourworldin data.org/democracy; Michael Doyle, "Liberalism and World Politics," *American Political Science Review* 80, no. 4 (December 1986): 1151–69.

37. Hal Brands, *American Grand Strategy and the Liberal Order: Continuity, Change, and Options for the Future* (Santa Monica: RAND, 2016), 3; Joshua P. Meltzer, "The Challenges to the World Trade Organization: It's All about Legitimacy," Brookings Institute, https://www.brookings.edu/research/the-challenges-to-the-world-trade-organization-its-all-about-legitimacy/.

38. Max Roser, "Economic Growth," Our World in Data, 2019, https://our worldindata.org/economic-growth; Michael J. Mazarr, Astrid Stuth Cevallos, Miranda Priebe, Andrew Radin, Kathleen Reedy, Alexander D. Rothenberg, Julia A. Thompson, and Jordan Wilcox, *Measuring the Health of the Liberal International Order* (Santa Monica: RAND, 2017), 62–64.

39. Roser, "Economic Growth"; Max Roser and Esteban Ortiz-Ospina, "Extreme Poverty," Our World in Data, 2019, https://ourworldindata.org/extreme-poverty.

40. Roser and Ortiz-Ospina, "Extreme Poverty"; Micah Zenko and Michael A. Cohen, "Clear and Present Safety," *Foreign Affairs* 91, no. 2 (March/April 2012): 79–93.

41. Robert Kagan, *The Jungle Grows Back: America and Our Imperiled World* (New York: Random House, 2019).

42. Mazarr et al., *Measuring the Health of the Liberal International Order*, 70; Burns H. Weston, "Security Council Resolution 678 and Persian Gulf Decision Making: Precarious Legitimacy," *American Journal of International Law* 85, no. 3 (July 1991): 516–35; Louis Fisher, "The Korean War: On What Legal Basis Did Truman Act?" *American Journal of International Law* 89, no. 1 (January 1995): 21–39.

43. Mearsheimer, "Bound to Fail," 23–24, 35; Charles Glaser, "A Flawed Framework: Why the Liberal International Order Concept Is Misguided," *International Security* 43, no. 4 (Spring 2019): 51–87.

44. Stephen M. Walt, "The Collapse of the Liberal World Order," *Foreign Policy*, June 26, 2018, https://foreignpolicy.com/2016/06/26/the-collapse-of-the-liberal-world-order-european-union-brexit-donald-trump/; Staniland, "Misreading the 'Liberal Order' "; Mearsheimer, "Bound to Fail," 23–24; Colgan and Keohane, "The Liberal Order Is Rigged."

45. Kagan, *The Jungle Grows Back*, 112–20, 135.

46. Kori Schake, *America versus the West: Can the Liberal World Order Be Preserved?* (Melbourne: Penguin Random House Australia, 2018), 12; Ivo H. Daalder and James M. Lindsay, "The Committee to Save the World Order: America's Allies Must Step Up as America Steps Down," *Foreign Affairs* 97, no. 6 (November/

December 2018): 72–83; Daniel Deudney and G. John Ikenberry, "Liberal World: The Resilient Order," *Foreign Affairs* 97, no. 4 (July/August 2018): 16–24.

47. G. John Ikenberry, "The Future of the Liberal World Order," *Foreign Affairs* 90, no. 3 (May/June 2011): 56–68.

48. Christopher Layne, *The Peace of Illusions: American Grand Strategy from 1940 to the Present* (Ithaca: Cornell University Press, 2007), 30.

49. John J. Mearsheimer and Stephen M. Walt, "The Case for Offshore Balancing: A Superior U.S. Grand Strategy," *Foreign Affairs* 95, no. 4 (July/August 2016): 70–83.

50. Brooks, Ikenberry, and Wohlforth, "Don't Come Home, America," 11; G. John Ikenberry, "The Plot against American Foreign Policy," *Foreign Affairs* 96, no. 3 (May/June 2017): 2–9.

51. Hal Brands, "The Pretty Successful Superpower," *American Interest*, November 2016, http://www.the-american-interest.com/2016/11/14/the-pretty-suc cessful-superpower/; Michael Beckley, *Unrivaled: Why America Will Remain the World's Sole Superpower* (Ithaca: Cornell University Press, 2018); Hal Brands and Eric Edelman, "Avoiding a Strategy of Bluff: The Crisis of American Military Primacy," Center for Strategic and Budgetary Assessments, 2017, http://csbaonline.org/uploads/documents/Strategic_Solvency_FINAL.pdf.

52. Bruce W. Jentleson, "Strategic Recalibration: Framework for a 21st-Century National Security Strategy," *Washington Quarterly* 37, no. 1 (2014): 115–36; Paul Stares, *Preventive Engagement: How America Can Avoid War, Stay Strong, and Keep the Peace* (New York: Columbia University Press, 2017); Anne-Marie Slaughter, *The Chessboard and the Web: Strategies of Connection in a Networked World* (New Haven: Yale University Press, 2017).

TWO

Domestic Disruptions

1. See, e.g., Shadi Hamid, "Trump and the Linkage of Domestic and Foreign Politics," *Brookings Order from Chaos*, November 9, 2016, https://www.brook ings.edu/blog/order-from-chaos/2016/11/09/trump-and-the-linkage-of-domestic-and-foreign-politics/; Julianne Smith, "Across the Pond, in the Field: Bringing U.S. Foreign Policy out of the Washington Bubble," Center for a New American Security, October 18, 2017, https://www.cnas.org/publi cations/commentary/across-the-pond-in-the-field-bringing-u-s-foreign-pol icy-out-of-the-washington-bubble; Heather Hurlburt, "Should We Take the 'Foreign' out of Foreign Policy?" New America, June 27, 2019, https://www. newamerica.org/weekly/edition-255/should-we-take-foreign-out-foreign-policy/.

2. Kurt M. Campbell, "How Income Inequality Undermines U.S. Power," *Washington Post*, November 28, 2014; Salman Ahmed et al., "U.S. Foreign Policy for

the Middle Class: Perspectives from Ohio," Carnegie Endowment for International Peace, December 10, 2018, https://carnegieendowment.org/2018/12/10/u.s.-foreign-policy-for-middle-class-perspectives-from-ohio-pub-77779; Heather Hurlburt, "Back to Basics: The Core Goals a 'Progressive' Foreign Policy Must Address," Policy Roundtable: The Future of Progressive Foreign Policy, *Texas National Security Review*, December 4, 2018, https://tnsr.org/roundtable/policy-roundtable-the-future-of-progressive-foreign-policy/#essay2.

3. American Association for the Advancement of Science, "Historical Trends in Federal R & D," last modified September 2019, https://www.aaas.org/programs/r-d-budget-and-policy/historical-trends-federal-rd.

4. Gregory Tassey, "A Technology-Based Growth Policy," *Issues in Science and Technology* 33, no. 2 (Winter 2017), https://issues.org/a-technology-based-growth-policy/; Jeffrey Mervis, "Data Check: U.S. Government Share of Basic Research Funding Falls Below 50%," *Science*, March 9, 2017, https://www.sciencemag.org/news/2017/03/data-check-us-government-share-basic-research-funding-falls-below 50; James Manyika, William H. McRaven, and Adam Segal, "Innovation and National Security: Keeping Our Edge," Independent Task Force Report no. 77, Council on Foreign Relations, 2019, 12, https://www.cfr.org/report/keeping-our-edge/pdf/TFR_Innovation_Strategy.pdf; Eric Schmidt et al., "Interim Report of the National Security Commission on Artificial Intelligence," National Security Commission on Artificial Intelligence, November 2019, 24–28, https://www.epic.org/foia/epic-v-ai-commission/AI-Commission-Interim-Report-Nov-2019.pdf.

5. World Bank, "Individuals Using the Internet (% of Population), East Asia & Pacific (1990–2018)," https://data.worldbank.org/indicator/IT.NET.USER.ZS?end=2018&locations=Z4&start=1990&view=chart.

6. Adam Segal, "Rebuilding Trust between Silicon Valley and Washington," Council on Foreign Relations, January 2017, 4–5, https://www.cfr.org/report/rebuilding-trust-between-silicon-valley-and-washington.

7. Alexis C. Madrigal, "Russia's Troll Operation Was Not That Sophisticated," *Atlantic*, February 19, 2018, https://www.theatlantic.com/technology/archive/2018/02/the-russian-conspiracy-to-commit-audience-development/553685/.

8. Adam Segal, *The Hacked World Order* (New York: Hachette Book Group, 2017), 280; Rachel Olney, "The Rift between Silicon Valley and the Pentagon Is Economic, Not Moral," *War on the Rocks*, January 28, 2019, https://warontherocks.com/2019/01/the-rift-between-silicon-valley-and-the-pentagon-is-economic-not-moral/.

9. Susie Allen, "The Double-Edged Sword of Government Funding," *STVP Stanford*, February 1, 2019, https://stvp.stanford.edu/blog/the-double-edged-sword-of-government-funding.

10. Future of Life Institute, "Lethal Autonomous Weapons Pledge," accessed January 12, 2020, https://futureoflife.org/lethal-autonomous-weapons-pledge/?cn-reloaded=1&cn-reloaded=1; Mark Bergen, "Google Staff AI Revolt Jeopardizes Pentagon Cloud Deals," *Bloomberg*, June 4, 2018, https://www.bloomberg.com/news/articles/2018-06-04/google-staff-ai-revolt-puts-pentagon-cloud-deals-in-jeopardy; Scott Shane, Cade Metz, and Daisuke Wakabayashi, "How a Pentagon Contract Became an Identity Crisis for Google," *New York Times*, May 30, 2018, https://www.nytimes.com/2018/05/30/technology/google-project-maven-pentagon.html.

11. Segal, "Rebuilding Trust between Silicon Valley and Washington," 8.

12. Danielle Abril, "This Is What Tech Companies Want in Any Federal Data Privacy Legislation," *Fortune*, February 21, 2019, https://fortune.com/2019/02/21/technology-companies-federal-data-privacy-law/.

13. Segal, *The Hacked World Order*, 279; Scott Thurm, "This Silicon Valley Lawmaker Has a Plan to Regulate Tech," *Wired*, April 30, 2018, https://www.wired.com/story/the-lawmaker-from-silicon-valley-who-wants-to-regulate-tech/; William D. Eggers, Mike Turley, and Pankaj Kishnani, "The Future of Regulation: Principles for Regulating Emerging Technologies," *Deloitte Insights*, June 19, 2018, https://www2.deloitte.com/us/en/insights/industry/public-sector/future-of-regulation/regulating-emerging-technology.html; Jamie Fly, Laura Rosenberger, and David Salvo, "European Policy Blueprint for Countering Authoritarian Influence in Democracies," Alliance for Securing Democracy, German Marshall Fund, 2019, 27, http://www.gmfus.org/publications/european-policy-blueprint-countering-authoritarian-interference-democracies.

14. Carroll Doherty, "7 Things to Know about Polarization in America," Pew Research Center, *FactTank*, June 12, 2014, http://www.pewresearch.org/fact-tank/2014/06/12/7-things-to-know-about-polarization-in-america/; Matthew Levendusky, *The Partisan Sort: How Liberals Became Democrats and Conservatives Became Republicans* (Chicago: University of Chicago Press, 2010); Ole R. Holsti, "Public Opinion and Foreign Policy: Challenges to the Almond-Lippmann Consensus," *International Studies Quarterly* 36, no. 4 (1992): 457–58.

15. Thomas Mann and Norman Ornstein, *It's Even Worse Than It Looks: How the American Constitutional System Collided with the New Politics of Extremism* (New York: Basic Books, 2012).

16. Matt Grossmann and David A. Hopkins, *Asymmetric Politics: Ideological Republicans and Group Interest Democrats* (New York: Oxford University Press, 2016), 258.

17. Kenneth Schultz, "The Perils of Polarization for U.S. Foreign Policy," *Washington Quarterly* 40, no. 4 (2018): 8; Nolan M. McCarty, Keith T. Poole, and Howard Rosenthal, *Polarized America: The Dance of Ideology and Unequal Riches* (Cambridge, MA: MIT Press, 2006); Doherty, "7 Things to Know about Polarization in America"; Shanto Iyengar, Gaurav Sood, and Yphtach Lelkes,

"Affect, Not Ideology: A Social Identity Perspective on Polarization," *Public Opinion Quarterly* 76, no. 3 (2012): 405–31; Lilliana Mason, " 'I Disrespectfully Agree': The Differential Effects of Partisan Sorting on Social and Issue Polarization," *American Journal of Political Science* 59, no. 1 (January 2015): 128–45; Alan I. Abramowitz and Steven Webster, "The Rise of Negative Partisanship and the Nationalization of U.S. Elections in the 21st Century," *Electoral Studies* 41 (March 2016): 12–22.

18. Anthony M. Bertelli and Jeffrey B. Wenger, "Demanding Information: Think Tanks and the U.S. Congress," *British Journal of Political Science* 39 (2008): 225–42.

19. Diana Epstein and John D. Graham, *Polarized Politics and Policy Consequences* (Santa Monica: RAND, 2007).

20. Schultz, "The Perils of Polarization for U.S. Foreign Policy"; Matthew A. Baum and Tim Groeling, "New Media and the Polarization of American Political Discourse," *Political Communication* 25, no. 4 (2008): 345–65.

21. However, some argue that the internet has had no impact on the amount of polarized news coverage consumed by the average American. See Matthew Gentzkow and Jesse M. Shapiro, "Ideological Segregation Online and Offline," NBER Working Paper Series, April 2010, https.//www.nber.org/papers/w15916.

22. Schultz, "The Perils of Polarization for U.S. Foreign Policy," 7–28.

23. James Fearon, "Signaling Foreign Policy Interests: Tying Hands versus Sinking Costs," *Journal of Conflict Resolution* 41, no. 1 (1997): 68–90; Branislav Slantchev, "Military Coercion in Interstate Crises," *American Political Science Review* 99, no. 4 (2005): 534; Branislav L. Slantchev, *Military Threats: The Costs of Coercion and the Price of Peace* (Cambridge: Cambridge University Press, 2011), 61, 78–80; Thomas C. Schelling, *Arms and Influence* (New Haven: Yale University Press, 1966); Robert L. Jervis, *The Logic of Images* (Princeton: Princeton University Press, 1970); Barry O'Neill, "The Intermediate Nuclear Force Missiles: An Analysis of Coupling and Reassurance," *International Interactions* 15, no. 3–4 (1990): 150; Michael Spence, "Job Market Signaling," *Quarterly Journal of Economics* 87, no. 3 (1973): 355–74.

24. E.g., William A. Galston, *Anti-Pluralism: The Populist Threat to Liberal Democracy* (New Haven: Yale University Press, 2017).

25. John Sides, Michael Tesler, and Lynn Vavreck, *Identity Crisis: The 2016 Presidential Campaign and the Meaning of America* (Princeton: Princeton University Press, 2018), 4–7; Campbell, "How Income Inequality Undermines U.S. Power"; Nat O'Connor, "Three Connections between Rising Economic Inequality and the Rise of Populism," *Irish Studies in International Affairs* 28 (2017): 29–43.

26. Raj Chetty et al., "Is the United States Still a Land of Opportunity? Recent Trends in Intergenerational Mobility," *American Economic Review: Papers and Proceedings* 104, no. 5 (2014): 141.

27. John Voorhees, Nolan McCarty, and Boris Shor, "Unequal Incomes, Ideology and Gridlock: How Rising Inequality Increases Political Polarization" (working paper, Washington Center for Equitable Growth, August 2015), http://ssrn.com/abstract=2649215.

28. Nolan McCarty, Keith T. Poole, and Howard Rosenthal, *Polarized America: The Dance of Ideology and Unequal Riches*, 2nd ed. (Cambridge, MA: MIT Press, 2016), chapters 1–2.

29. John Voorheis, Nolan McCarty, and Boris Shor, "Unequal Incomes, Ideology and Gridlock: How Rising Inequality Increases Political Polarization" (working paper, NYU Law, March 16, 2016), http://www.law.nyu.edu/sites/default/files/upload_documents/Nolan%20McCarty%20Paper%20Polarization_draft_shared%20031616.pdf.

30. Chicago Council on Global Affairs, "Rejecting Retreat," September 6, 2019, https://www.thechicagocouncil.org/publication/rejecting-retreat.

31. Campbell, "How Income Inequality Undermines U.S. Power"; O'Connor, "Three Connections between Rising Economic Inequality and the Rise of Populism"; Sides, Tesler, and Vavreck, *Identity Crisis*, 4–7.

32. Robert J. Blendon, Logan S. Casey, and John M. Benson, "Public Opinion and Trump's Jobs and Trade Policies," *Challenge* 60, no. 3 (2017): 228–44; Carl Benedikt Frey and Michael A. Osborne, "The Future of Employment: How Susceptible Are Jobs to Computerisation?" *Technological Forecasting and Social Change* 114 (January 2017): 254–80; Melanie Arntz, Terry Gregory, and Ulrich Zierahn, "The Risk of Automation for Jobs in OECD Countries," OECD Social, Employment and Migration Working Papers no. 189, June 16, 2016, https://www.oecd-ilibrary.org/social-issues-migration-health/the-risk-of-automation-for-jobs-in-oecd-countries_5jlz9h56dvq7-en; David H. Autor, "Why Are There Still So Many Jobs? The History and Future of Automation," *Journal of Economic Perspectives* 29, no. 3 (Summer 2015): 3–30; Bureau of Labor Statistics, "Employment Projections, 2016–2016," October 24, 2017, https://www.bls.gov/news.release/pdf/ecopro.pdf.

33. Adam Tooze, *Crashed: How a Decade of Financial Crises Changed the World* (New York: Viking, 2018), 28–29; Congressional Budget Office, *The Budget and Economic Outlook, 2018 to 2028*, April 9, 2018, https://www.cbo.gov/publication/53651; James McBride and Jonathan Masters, "The National Debt Dilemma," Council on Foreign Relations, May 2018, https://www.cfr.org/backgrounder/national-debt-dilemma.

34. Kate Davidson and Daniel Kruger, "US on a Course to Spend More on Debt Than Defense," *Wall Street Journal*, November 11, 2018.

35. Jason Furman and Lawrence H. Summers, "Who's Afraid of Budget Deficits? How Washington Should End Its Debt Obsession," *Foreign Affairs* 98, no. 2 (March/April 2019): 82–95; Joe Gould, "Bolton: National Debt 'Threat to Society,' Forcing DoD Spending to 'Flatten Out,' " *Defense News*, November 1, 2018.

36. Todd Harrison and Seamus P. Daniels, *Analysis of the 2019 Defense Budget* (Washington, DC: CSIS, 2018); Todd Harrison, *Defense Modernization Plans through the 2020s: Addressing the Bow Wave* (Washington, DC: CSIS, 2016).

37. Barry Eichengreen, *Exorbitant Privilege: The Rise and Fall of the Dollar and the Future of the International Monetary System* (New York: Oxford University Press, 2012), 162.

38. Raymond Zhong, "China's Cryptocurrency Plan Has a Powerful Partner: Big Brother," *New York Times*, October 18, 2019, https://www.nytimes.com/2019/10/18/technology/china-cryptocurrency-facebook-libra.html.

39. Joshua A. Tucker, Yannis Theocharis, Margaret E. Roberts, and Pablo Barbera, "From Liberation to Turmoil: Social Media and Democracy," *Journal of Democracy* 26, no. 4 (2017): 46–59; Scott Shane, "The Fakes the Russians Created to Influence the Election," *New York Times*, September 7, 2017; Craig Silverman, "This Analysis Shows How Viral Fake Election News Stories Outperformed Real News on Facebook," *BuzzFeed*, November 16, 2016; Katie Rogers and Jonah Engel Bromwich, "The Hoaxes, Fake News, and Misinformation We Saw on Election Day," *New York Times*, November 8, 2016; Craig Timberg, "Russian Propaganda Effort Helped Spread 'Fake News' during Election, Experts Say," *Washington Post*, November 24, 2016.

40. Cass R. Sunstein, *#Republic: Divided Democracy in the Age of Social Media* (Princeton: Princeton University Press, 2017); B.E. Weeks, "Emotions, Partisanship, and Misperceptions: How Anger and Anxiety Moderate the Effect of Partisan Bias on Susceptibility to Political Misinformation," *Journal of Communication* 65, no. 4 (2015): 699–719; Iyengar, Sood, and Lelkes, "Affect, Not Ideology."

41. Larry Diamond, Marc F. Plattner, and Christopher Walker, *Authoritarianism Goes Global: The Challenge to Democracy* (Baltimore: Johns Hopkins University Press, 2016); Tucker, Theocharis, Roberts, and Barbera, "From Liberation to Turmoil: Social Media and Democracy."

42. Clint Watts, *Messing with the Enemy: Surviving in a Social Media World of Hackers, Terrorists, Russians, and Fake News* (New York: Harper, 2018).

THREE

Power, Technology, and a World in Flux

1. Charles Krauthammer, "The Unipolar Moment," *Foreign Affairs* 70, no. 1 (1990–91): 23–33.

2. Joseph Nye, *Soft Power: The Means to Success in World Politics* (New York: PublicAffairs, 2005).

3. Robert Keohane and Joseph Nye, *Power and Interdependence* (Boston: Little, Brown, 1977); Emilie M. Hafner-Burton, Miles Kahler, and Alexander H. Montgomery, "Network Analysis for International Relations," *International Organization* 63, no. 3 (July 2009): 559–592; Henry Farrell and Abraham L.

Newman, "Weaponized Interdependence: How Global Economic Networks Shape State Coercion," *International Security* 44, no. 1 (Summer 2019): 42–79.

4. Oriana Skylar Mastro, "The Stealth Superpower: How China Hid Its Global Ambitions," *Foreign Affairs* 98, no. 1 (January/February 2019), foreignaffairs.com/articles/china/china-plan-rule-asia.

5. World Bank Group, "Global Economic Prospects: The Turning of the Tide?" June 2018, https://elibrary.worldbank.org/doi/pdf/10.1596/978-1-4648-1257-6; Cao Jing and Mun Ho, "China: Economic and GHG Emissions Outlook to 2050," Global Commission on the Economy and Climate, September 15, 2014, 28, https://scholar.harvard.edu/files/munho/files/cao-ho.sep2014.pdf. Note that China already has the world's largest economy by purchasing power parity; see Organization for Economic Cooperation and Development, "Gross Domestic Product," *OECD Data*, 2018, https://data.oecd.org/gdp/gross-domestic-product-gdp.htm; Duncan Clark, "China Is Shaping the Future of Global Tech," *Financial Times*, January 12, 2018.

6. Kevin Zraick, "China Will Feel One-Child Policy's Effects for Decades, Experts Say," *New York Times*, October 30, 2015, https://www.nytimes.com/2015/10/31/world/asia/china-will-feel-one-child-policys-effects-for-decades-experts-say.html; Quanbao Jiang, Shucai Yang, and Jesús J. Sánchez-Barricarte, "Can China Afford Rapid Aging?" *Springerplus* 5, no. 1 (2016), https://www.ncbi.nlm.nih.gov/pmc/articles/PMC4949193/; Scott Neuman and Robert Schmitz, "Despite the End of China's One-Child Policy, Births Are Still Lagging," *NPR*, July 16, 2018, https://www.npr.org/2018/07/16/629361870/despite-the-end-of-chinas-one-child-policy-births-are-still-lagging.

7. Michael Beckley, "The Emerging Military Balance in East Asia: How China's Neighbors Can Check China's Naval Expansion," *International Security* 42, no. 2 (Fall 2017): 78–119; Michael Beckley, *Unrivaled: Why America Will Remain the World's Sole Superpower* (Ithaca: Cornell University Press, 2018), chapters 2–3.

8. Andrew J. Nathan, "The Chinese World Order," *New York Review*, October 12, 2017, https://www.nybooks.com/articles/2017/10/12/chinese-world-order/; Andrew F. Krepinevich, "Maritime Competition in a Mature Precision-Strike Regime," CSBA, April 2015, http://csbaonline.org/publications/2015/04/maritime-competition-in-a-mature-precision-strike-regime/; Thomas G. Mahnken, "Weapons: The Growth & Spread of the Precision-Strike Regime," *Daedalus* 140, no. 3 (Summer 2011): 45–57; Aaron Friedberg, *Beyond Air-Sea Battle: The Debate over US Military Strategy in Asia* (London: International Institute for Strategic Studies, 2014).

9. U.S.-China Economic and Security Review Commission, *PLA Military Modernization: Drivers, Force Restructuring, and Implications*, February 15, 2018, statement of Cortez A. Cooper III, RAND, 1–2, https://www.rand.org/pubs/testimonies/CT488.html; Michael S. Chase et al., "China's Incomplete Military Transformation: Assessing the Weaknesses of the People's Liberation Army (PLA)," RAND, 2015, https://www.rand.org/content/dam/rand/pubs/

research_reports/RR800/RR893/RAND_RR893.pdf; Joel Wuthnow and Phillip C. Saunders, "Chinese Military Reform in the Age of Xi Jinping: Drivers, Challenges, and Implications," Center for the Study of Chinese Military Affairs, Institute for National Strategic Studies, March 2017, https://ndupress. ndu.edu/Portals/68/Documents/stratperspective/china/ChinaPerspec tives-10.pdf; Chase et al., "China's Incomplete Military Transformation"; U.S.-China Economic and Security Review Commission, *PLA Military Modernization*; Eric Heginbotham et al., "U.S.-China Military Scorecard: Forces, Geography, and the Evolving Balance of Power, 1996–2017," RAND, 2015, https://www.rand.org/content/dam/rand/pubs/research_reports/RR300/ RR392/RAND_RR392.pdf; Michael J. Green, Kathleen H. Hicks, John Schaus, Zack Cooper, and Jake Douglas, *Countering Coercion in Maritime Asia: The Theory and Practice of Gray Zone Deterrence* (Washington, DC: Center for Strategic and International Studies, 2017), https://www.csis.org/analysis/ countering-coercion-maritime-asia.

10. Dmitri Trenin, *Post-Imperium: A Eurasian Story* (Washington, DC: Carnegie Endowment for International Peace, 2011); Andrew C. Kuchins and Igor A. Zevelev, "Russian Foreign Policy: Continuity in Change," *Washington Quarterly* 35, no. 1 (2012): 147–61; Celeste Wallander, "Russian Transimperialism and Its Implications," *Washington Quarterly* 30, no. 2 (2007): 107–22; Brian D. Taylor, *The Code of Putinism* (Oxford: Oxford University Press, 2018).

11. Stolypin Club, *Strategii rosta* [Growth Strategies] (Moscow: Stolypin Club, Centre for Strategic Research, 2017). The World Bank estimates oil prices will hover around $70 per barrel by 2030. World Bank, "Commodity Markets Outlook," April 24, 2018, https://www.worldbank.org/en/research/commodity-markets#3; PricewaterhouseCoopers, "The Long View: How Will the Global Economic Order Change by 2050?" February 2017, https://www.pwc.com/gx/ en/issues/economy/the-world-in-2050.html; Michael Kofman and Richard Connolly, "Why Russian Military Expenditure Is Much Higher Than Commonly Understood (as is China's)," *War on the Rocks*, December 16, 2019, https://warontherocks.com/2019/12/why-russian-military-expenditure-is-much-higher-than-commonly-understood-as-is-chinas/.

12. Richard Connolly and Mathieu Boulègue, "Russia's New State Armament Programme: Implications for the Russian Armed Forces and Military Capabilities to 2027," Chatham House, May 2018, 15, https://www.chathamhouse. org/sites/default/files/publications/research/2018-05-10-russia-state-arma ment-programme-connolly-boulegue-final.pdf. On cyber and hybrid war, see Molly K. McKew, "The Gerasimov Doctrine," *Politico*, September 5, 2017, https://www.politico.eu/article/new-battles-cyberwarfare-russia/; Sarah P. White, "Understanding Cyberwarfare," Modern War Institute at West Point, March 20, 2018, 1–28, https://mwi.usma.edu/wp-content/uploads/2018/03/ Understanding-Cyberwarfare.pdf; Stephen Blank, "Cyber War and Information War à La Russe," in *Understanding Cyber Conflict: Fourteen Analogies*, ed.

George Perkovich and Ariel E. Levite (Washington, DC: Georgetown University Press, 2017). On nuclear, see James T. Quinlivan and Olga Oliker, "Nuclear Deterrence in Europe," RAND, 2011, https://www.rand.org/pubs/monographs/MG1075.html; Nikolai Sokov, "Why Russia Calls a Limited Nuclear Strike 'De-escalation,' " *Bulletin of the Atomic Scientists*, March 13, 2014, https://thebulletin.org/2014/03/why-russia-calls-a-limited-nuclear-strike-de-escalation/; Elbridge Colby, "Nuclear Weapons in the Third Offset Strategy: Avoiding a Nuclear Blind Spot in the Pentagon's New Initiative," Center for a New American Security, February 2015, https://www.cnas.org/publications/reports/nuclear-weapons-in-the-third-offset-strategy-avoiding-a-nuclear-blind-spot-in-the-pentagons-new-initiative; Matthew Kroenig, "The Renewed Russian Nuclear Threat and NATO Nuclear Deterrence Posture," Issue Brief, Atlantic Council, February 2016, http://www.matthewkroenig.com/Kroenig_Russian_Nuclear_Threat.pdf; Olga Oliker, "Russia's Nuclear Doctrine: What We Know, What We Don't, and What That Means," Center for Strategic and International Studies, May 2016, 14, https://csis-prod.s3.amazonaws.com/s3fs-public/publication/160504_Oliker_RussiasNuclear-Doctrine_Web.pdf; Kristin Ven Bruusgaard, "The Myth of Russia's Lowered Nuclear Threshold," *War on the Rocks*, September 22, 2017, https://warontherocks.com/2017/09/the-myth-of-russias-lowered-nuclear-threshold/; Bruno Tertrais, "Russia's Nuclear Policy: Worrying for the Wrong Reasons," *Survival* 60, no. 2 (2018): 33–44.

13. Ihor Kabanenko, "Russian Blue Water Ambitions: Betting on Multi-purpose Frigates," Jamestown Foundation, May 12, 2017, https://jamestown.org/program/russian-blue-water-ambitions-betting-multi-purpose-frigates/.

14. PricewaterhouseCoopers, "The Long View."

15. Beckley, *Unrivaled*, chapters 2–3; Eric Schmidt et al., "Interim Report of the National Security Commission on Artificial Intelligence," National Security Commission on Artificial Intelligence, November 2019, 24–28, https://www.epic.org/foia/epic-v-ai-commission/AI-Commission-Interim-Report-Nov-2019.pdf.

16. A reserve currency is one held in large quantities by central banks and other financial institutions to prepare for investments, transactions, and international debt obligations, or to influence the country's domestic exchange rate. See James Chen, "Reserve Currency," Investopedia, updated February 7, 2018, https://www.investopedia.com/terms/r/reservecurrency.asp; Barry Eichengreen, *Exorbitant Privilege: The Rise and Fall of the Dollar and the Future of the International Monetary System* (New York: Oxford University Press, 2012), 127–29; Richard Dobbs et al., "An Exorbitant Privilege? Implications of Reserve Currencies for Competitiveness," McKinsey & Company, 2009, 16, https://www.mckinsey.com/~/media/McKinsey/Featured%20Insights/Global%20Capital%20Markets/An%20exorbitant%20privilege/MGI_An_exorbitant_privilege_Implications%20of%20reserve_currencies_full_discussion_paper.

ashx; Jeffrey Frankel, "The Rise of the Renminbi as International Currency: Historical Precedents," VoxEU.Org, October 10, 2011, https://voxcu.org/article/rise-renminbi-international-currency-historical-precedents.

17. Satyajit Das, "How the U.S. Has Weaponized the Dollar," *Bloomberg*, September 6, 2018, https://www.bloomberg.com/view/articles/2018-09-06/how-the-u-s-has-made-a-weapon-of-the-dollar; Farrell and Newman, "Weaponized Interdependence."

18. Congressional Budget Office, "10-Year Budget and Economic Data," April 2018, https://www.cbo.gov/about/products/budget-economic-data#4; Jonathan Caverley, "America's Arms Sales Policy: Security Abroad, Not Jobs at Home," *War on the Rocks*, April 6, 2018, https://warontherocks.com/2018/04/americas-arms-sales-policy-security-abroad-not-jobs-at-home/.

19. "National Defense Strategy of the United States of America," Department of Defense, 2018, https://dod.defense.gov/Portals/1/Documents/pubs/2018-National-Defense-Strategy-Summary.pdf; Joseph Nye Jr., "The Future of American Power," *Foreign Affairs*, November/December 2010, https://www.foreignaffairs.com/articles/2010-11-01/future-american-power; Stephen Brooks and William Wohlforth, "The Once and Future Superpower: Why China Won't Overtake the United States," *Foreign Affairs* 95, no. 3 (May/June 2016): 91–104.

20. European Commission, "2018 Ageing Report," November 2017, https://ec.europa.eu/info/sites/info/files/economy-finance/ip065_en.pdf; UN Population Data, accessed January 13, 2020, https://population.un.org/wpp/DataQuery/.

21. Matilde Mas et al., "The 2018 PREDICT Key Facts Report: An Analysis of ICT R&D in the EU and Beyond," JRC Technical Reports, European Commission, 2018, https://ec.europa.eu/jrc/sites/jrcsh/files/jrc111895.pdf; "Brexit-Related Concerns Remain Key for UK Tech, Says UK Gov Report," *TechCrunch*, accessed October 8, 2018, http://social.techcrunch.com/2018/05/17/brexit-related-concerns-remain-key-for-uk-tech-says-uk-gov-report/; Cornelius McGrath, "Move to Silicon Valley Vital for Ambitious European Tech Groups," *Financial Times*, November 23, 2017, https://www.ft.com/content/33a85426-6277-11e7-8814-0ac7eb84e5f1.

22. Organization for Economic Cooperation and Development, "GDP Long-Term Forecast," last updated 2018, https://data.oecd.org/gdp/gdp-long-term-forecast.htm; World Bank, "DataBank," last updated December 31, 2019, https://databank.worldbank.org/home.aspx; Organization for Economic Cooperation and Development, "Data," accessed January 13, 2020; National Institute of Population and Social Security Research, "Population Projections for Japan (2017): 2016 to 2065," 2017, http://fpcj.jp/wp/wp-content/uploads/2017/04/1db9de3ea4ade06c3023d3ba54dd98of.pdf; Choi He-suk, "South Korea 2030—A New Society with New Challenges," *Korea Herald*, August 16, 2017; Infrastructure Australia, "Population Estimates and Projections," April

2015, https://www.infrastructureaustralia.gov.au/sites/default/files/2019-07/Background-paper-on-demographic-projections.pdf; Tim Romero, "It Won't Be Japan's Startups That Revive the Country's Innovation, but Its Mid-sized Tech Firms," *Forbes*, November 27, 2017, https://www.forbes.com/sites/outofasia/2017/11/27/it-wont-be-japans-startups-that-revive-the-countrys-innovation-but-its-mid-sized-tech-firms/#3ffaa9dc7e21; Ingo Beyer von Morgenstern, Peter Kenevan, and Ulrich Naeher, "Rebooting Japan's High-Tech Sector," *McKinsey Quarterly*, June 2011; World Bank, "DataBank."

23. Crystal Pryor and Tom Le, "Looking beyond 1 Percent: Japan's Security Expenditures," *Diplomat*, April 3, 2018, https://thediplomat.com/2018/04/looking-beyond-1-percent-japans-security-expenditures/; Hal Brands, "Dealing with Allies in Decline: Alliance Management and U.S. Strategy in an Era of Global Power Shifts," Center for Strategic and Budgetary Assessments, 2017, https://csbaonline.org/uploads/documents/ALLIES_in_DECLINE_FINAL_b.pdf.

24. Brands, "Dealing with Allies in Decline."

25. Kathleen H. Hicks et al., "Counting Dollars or Measuring Value? Assessing NATO and Partner Burden Sharing," Center for Strategic and International Studies, July 2018, https://csis-prod.s3.amazonaws.com/s3fs-public/publication/180703_Hicks_CountingDollars.pdf?ODJoCMVuu4utZMU.R1Y14E-Fdp.ma7JEc; Richard Fontaine, Patrick M. Cronin, Mira Rapp-Hooper, and Harry Krejsa, *Networked Asian Security: An Integrated Approach to Order in the Pacific* (Washington, DC: Center for a New American Security, 2017); Michael Heazel and Andrew O'Neill, eds., *China's Rise and US-Japan-Australia Relations: Primacy and Leadership in East Asia* (London: Edward Elgar, 2018).

26. PricewaterhouseCoopers, "The Long View."

27. Organization for Economic Cooperation and Development, "GDP Long-Term Forecast"; Benoit Guerin et al., "A Growing and Ageing Population: Global Societal Trends to 2030, Thematic Report 1" (Santa Monica: RAND, 2015); IISS, *The Military Balance, 2018*, 2018, https://www.iiss.org/publications/the-military-balance/the-military-balance-2018; "India's 'Cold Start' Doctrine: All You Need to Know," *Times of India*, September 21, 2017, https://timesofindia.indiatimes.com/india/indias-cold-start-doctrine-all-you-need-to-know/articleshow/60775111.cms; Stephen Cohen and Sunil Dasgupta, *Arming without Aiming: India's Military Modernization* (Washington, DC: Brookings Institution Press, 2010), 36–37; Brigadier Mick Ryan, Australian Army, "India-China in 2030: A Net Assessment of the Competition between Two Rising Powers," Ministry of Defense of Australia, October 2012, 39, https://www.defence.gov.au/ADC/Publications/documents/Commanders/2012/Ryan-2012.pdf; Daniel Kliman, Iskander Rehman, Kristine Lee, and Joshua Fitt, *Imbalance of Power: India's Military Choices in an Era of Strategic Competition with China* (Washington, DC: Center for a New American Security, 2019), https://www.cnas.org/publications/reports/imbalance-of-power.

28. PricewaterhouseCoopers, "The Long View"; World Bank Group, "Global Economic Prospects"; Central Intelligence Agency, *The World Factbook*, accessed January 13, 2020, https://www.cia.gov/library/publications/the-world-factbook/fields/print_2103.html; Laura Noonan, "Vietnam's Nascent Debt Markets Set for Bigger Deals," *Financial Times*, December 13, 2017, https://www.ft.com/content/5a28f5ee-dfe3-11e7-8f9f-de1c2175f5ce; Le Vinh Trien and Kris Hartley, "Doi Moi II: Rule of Law and State Legitimacy in Vietnam," *Diplomat*, July 14, 2017, https://thediplomat.com/2017/07/doi-moi-ii-rule-of-law-and-state-legitimacy-in-vietnam/; Vivienne Nunis, "Could Vietnam Become the Next Silicon Valley?" *BBC News*, February 2, 2016, https://www.bbc.com/news/business-35227626.

29. PricewaterhouseCoopers, "The Long View"; World Bank, "DataBank"; IHS Markit, "Emerging Markets in Asia Pacific Offer Brightest Prospects for Global FDI, IHS Study Finds," IHS Online Newsroom, https://news.ihsmarkit.com/press-release/economics-country-risk/emerging-markets-asia-pacific-offer-brightest-prospects-global-; Euromonitor International, "Philippines in 2030: The Future Demographic," December 2017, https://www.euromonitor.com/philippines-in-2030-the-future-demographic/report; Oliver Segovia, "How the Philippines Became Tech Startups' New Source for Talent," *Harvard Business Review*, August 5, 2015, https://hbr.org/2015/08/how-the-philippines-became-tech-startups-new-source-for-talent; SIPRI, *SIPRI Military Expenditure Database*, https://www.sipri.org/databases/milex.

30. Adam Segal, *Advantage: How American Innovation Can Overcome the Asian Challenge* (New York: Norton, 2012); Schmidt et al., "Interim Report of the National Security Commission on Artificial Intelligence."

31. Kai-Fu Lee, *AI Superpowers: China, Silicon Valley, and the New World Order* (New York: Houghton Mifflin, 2018).

32. Charles Rollet, "The Odd Reality of Life under China's All-Seeing Credit Score System," *Wired*, June 5, 2018, http://www.wired.co.uk/article/china-social-credit; Simina Mistreaun, "Life inside China's Social Credit Laboratory," *Foreign Policy*, April 3, 2018, https://foreignpolicy.com/2018/04/03/life-inside-chinas-social-credit-laboratory/.

33. Nicholas Wright, "How Artificial Intelligence Will Reshape the Global Order," *Foreign Affairs*, July 10, 2018, https://www.foreignaffairs.com/articles/world/2018-07-10/how-artificial-intelligence-will-reshape-global-order; "Saudi Arabia," *Freedom on the Net 2017*, Freedom House, 2017, https://freedomhouse.org/report/freedom-net/2017/saudi-arabia; "UAE: Authorities Enhance Surveillance of Critics," Human Rights Watch, January 12, 2017, https://www.hrw.org/news/2017/01/12/uae-authorities-enhance-surveillance-critics; Daniel Moritz-Rabson, "Egypt Passes New Restrictions on Free Press, Social Media," *Newsweek*, July 18, 2018, https://www.newsweek.com/egypt-passes-new-restrictions-free-press-1031784; Bassem Aboualabass and Aziz El

Massassi, "Egypt Looks to Monitor Popular Social Media Users," AFP, June 28, 2018, https://www.yahoo.com/news/egypt-looks-monitor-popular-social-me dia-users-025914016.html; Angus Berwick, "How ZTE Helps Venezuela Create China-Style Social Control," Reuters, November 14, 2018, https://www. reuters.com/investigates/special-report/venezuela-zte/. See, e.g., Louise Lucas, "The Chinese Communist Party Entangles Big Tech," *Financial Times*, July 19, 2018; Chris Balding, "China Is Nationalizing Its Tech Sector," *Bloomberg*, April 11, 2018; Louise Lucas, "Beijing's Battle to Control Its Home-grown Tech Giants," *Financial Times*, September 23, 2017; Elizabeth C. Economy, *Xi Jinping and the Third Revolution* (Oxford: Oxford University Press, 2018), 123.

34. Hal Brands, "Democracy vs Authoritarianism," *Survival* 60, no. 5 (2018): 79, 83, 86; Adam Segal, "Chinese Cyber Diplomacy in a New Era of Uncertainty," Stanford University Hoover Institution Aegis Paper Series no. 1703, 11–14, https://www.hoover.org/sites/default/files/research/docs/segal_chinese_ cyber_diplomacy.pdf.

35. Michael Horowitz, "Artificial Intelligence, International Competition, and the Balance of Power," *Texas National Security Review* 1, no. 3 (May 2018): 36–57.

36. "Impact of Unmanned Systems to Escalation Dynamics," CNA, 2018, https:// www.cna.org/CNA_files/PDF/Summary-Impact-of-Unmanned-Systems-to-Escalation-Dynamics.pdf.

37. Adam Segal, *The Hacked World Order* (New York: Hachette Book Group, 2017), 53.

FOUR

The Contest for Twenty-First-Century Order

1. Michael J. Mazarr, Timothy R. Heath, and Astrid Stuth Cevallos, *China and the International Order* (Santa Monica: RAND, 2018), 32.

2. On China in the UN system: Andrew J. Nathan, "China's Rise and International Regimes: Does China Seek to Overthrow Global Norms?" in *China in the Era of Xi Jinping: Domestic and Foreign Policy Challenges*, ed. Robert S. Ross and Jo Inge Bekkevold (Washington, DC: Georgetown University Press, 2016), 171. On China and human rights regimes: Mazarr, Heath, and Cevallos, *China and the International Order*, 30–31; Zhou Qi, "Conflicts over Human Rights between China and the US," *Human Rights Quarterly* 27, no. 1 (2005): 105–24; Associated Press, "Human Rights in China under Xi Worst since Tiananmen: Amnesty," *South China Morning Post*, November 17, 2017; Kata Isenring-Szabó, "China's Views on the Human Rights Council," in *The United Nations of China: A Vision of the World Order* (Brussels: European Council on Foreign Relations, 2018); Sophie Richardson, "Is China Winning Its Fight against Rights at the UN?" *The Hill*, December 12, 2018; Jessica Chen Weiss, "A World Safe for Autocracy? China's Rise and the Future of Global Politics," *Foreign Affairs* 98, no. 4 (July/August 2019): 92–108.

3. Jose De Gregorio et al., *IMF Reform: The Unfinished Agenda* (Geneva: International Center for Monetary and Banking Studies, 2018), section 5.4.
4. Catherine Cadell, "China's Xi Urges Cooperation among Nations in Governance of Global Internet," Reuters, November 16, 2016, https://www.reuters.com/article/us-china-internet/chinas-xi-urges-cooperation-among-nations-in-governance-of-global-internet-idUSKBN13B1FF; Dan Levin, "At U.N., China Tries to Influence Fight over Internet Control," *New York Times*, December 17, 2015; Hilary McGeachy, *US-China Technology Competition: Impacting a Rules-Based Order* (Sydney: United States Studies Center at the University of Sydney, 2019); Anthea Roberts, Henrique Choer Moraes, and Victor Ferguson, "Geoeconomics: The Chinese Strategy of Technological Advancement and Cybersecurity," *Lawfare*, December 3, 2018, https://www.lawfareblog.com/geoeconomics-chinese-strategy-technological-advancement-and-cybersecurity.
5. Elizabeth C. Economy, "Why China Is No Climate Leader," *Politico*, June 12, 2017; Christina Nunez, "China Poised for Leadership on Climate Change After U.S. Reversal," *National Geographic*, March 28, 2017; Elizabeth Economy, *The River Runs Black* (Ithaca: Cornell University Press, 2004); Eleanor Albert and Beina Xu, "China's Environmental Crisis," Council on Foreign Relations Backgrounder, January 18, 2016, https://www.cfr.org/backgrounder/chinas-environmental-crisis.
6. Chinese Consulate General in Karachi, "The Five Principles of Peaceful Coexistence," Ministry of Foreign Affairs of the People's Republic of China, July 3, 2014, https://www.fmprc.gov.cn/mfa_eng/wjb_663304/zwjg_665342/zwbd_665378/t1179045.shtml; John Ruwitch, "China's Xi Issues Veiled Warning to Asia over Military Alliances," Reuters, May 20, 2014, https://www.reuters.com/article/us-china-xi/chinas-xi-issues-veiled-warning-to-asia-over-military-alliances-idUSBREA4K02V20140521; Adam P. Liff, "China and the US Alliance System," *China Quarterly* 233 (March 2018): 137–65; Mazarr, Heath, and Cevallos, *China and the International Order*, 29.
7. On the SCO: Eleanor Albert, "The Shanghai Cooperation Organization," Council on Foreign Relations Backgrounder, October 14, 2015, https://www.cfr.org/backgrounder/shanghai-cooperation-organization; Julie Boland, *Ten Years of the Shanghai Cooperation Organization: A Lost Decade? A Partner for the United States?* (Washington, DC: Brookings Institution Press, 2011); Catherine Putz, "A West in Crisis, an East Rising? Comparing the G7 and the SCO," *Diplomat*, June 12, 2018, https://thediplomat.com/2018/06/a-west-in-crisis-an-east-rising-comparing-the-g7-and-the-sco/; Felix Chang, "Organization of Rivals: Limits of the Shanghai Cooperation Organization," Foreign Policy Research Institute, September 27, 2018, https://www.fpri.org/article/2018/09/organization-of-rivals-limits-of-the-shanghai-cooperation-organization/. On the AIIB: Asian Infrastructure and Investment Bank, *Financing Asia's Future: 2017 AIIB Annual Report and Financials* (Beijing: Asian Infrastructure Investment Bank, 2018); Tamar Gutner, "AIIB: Is the Chinese-Led Development

Bank a Role Model?" Council on Foreign Relations, June 25, 2018, https://www.cfr.org/blog/aiib-chinese-led-development-bank-role-model.

8. Andrew Chatzky and James McBride, "China's Massive Belt and Road Initiative," Council on Foreign Relations Backgrounder, May 21, 2019, https://www.cfr.org/backgrounder/chinas-massive-belt-and-road-initiative; Jonathan Hillman, *The Emperor's New Road* (New Haven: Yale University Press, 2020), 11–12, chapters 3–8; Saeed Shah, "China's Belt-and-Road Initiative Puts a Squeeze on Pakistan," *Wall Street Journal*, April 3, 2019; Jeremy Page and Saeed Shah, "China's Global Building Spree Runs into Trouble in Pakistan," *Wall Street Journal*, July 22, 2018; Andrew Chatzky, "China's Belt and Road Gets a Win in Italy," Council on Foreign Relations, March 27, 2019, https://www.cfr.org/in-brief/chinas-belt-and-road-gets-win-italy; Nadege Rolland, *China's Eurasian Century? Political and Strategic Implications of the Belt and Road Initiative* (Washington, DC: National Bureau of Asia Research, 2017); U.S.-China Economic and Security Review Commission, *China's Belt and Road Initiative: Five Years Later*, January 25, 2018, statement of Jonathan E. Hillman, Center for Strategic and International Studies, https://www.csis.org/analysis/chinas-belt-and-road-initiative-five-years-later-0; Jonathan Hillman and Matthew Goodman, "All Rise? Belt and Road Court Is in Session," Center for Strategic and International Studies, July 26, 2018, https://www.csis.org/analysis/all-rise-belt-and-road-court-session.

9. Michael Kofman, "Raiding and International Brigandry: Russia's Strategy for Great Power Competition," *War on the Rocks*, June 14, 2018, https://warontherocks.com/2018/06/raiding-and-international-brigandry-russias-strategy-for-great-power-competition/; Richard Sakawa, *Russia against the West: The Post–Cold War Crisis of World Order* (Cambridge: Cambridge University Press, 2017), 48; Angela E. Stent, *Putin's World: Russia against the West and with the Rest* (New York: Hachette Book Group, 2019), 349–50; Stephen Kotkin, "Russia's Perpetual Geopolitics: Putin Returns to the Historical Pattern," *Foreign Affairs* 95, no. 2 (May/June 2016): 2–9.

10. Andrew Radin and Clint Reach, *Russian Views of the International Order* (Santa Monica: RAND, 2015), 36; Yiqin Fu, "UN View: United Nations General Assembly Voting Patterns (1946–2019)," https://dataviz.yiqinfu.com/unview/.

11. Dimitri Trenin, "Russia's New National Strategy," Carnegie Europe, August 22, 2014, https://carnegieeurope.eu/strategiceurope/56442.

12. On modernization: Pamela A. Jordan, "Diminishing Returns: Russia's Participation in the World Trade Organization," *Post-Soviet Affairs* 33, no. 6 (2017): 452–71; Richard Connolly, "Economic Modernisation in Russia: The Role of the World Trade Organization," *European Politics and Society* 16, no. 1 (2015): 27–44; Richard Connolly and Philip Hanson, "Russia's Accession to the World Trade Organization: Commitments, Processes, and Prospects," *Eurasian Geography and Economics* 53, no. 4 (2012): 479–501; United States Trade Representative, *2018 Report on the Implementation and Enforcement of Russia's WTO*

Commitments (Washington, DC: U.S. Trade Representative, 2019). On trade policy: Radin and Reach, *Russian Views of the International Order,* 56–57; Dipanjan Chaudhury, "India, Russia Plan Free Trade Agreement in Eurasian Region," *Economic Times,* May 29, 2017; Anthony Rinna, "Here Is Why South Korea May Be Turning to Russia," *National Interest,* February 6, 2018.

13. On cyber sovereignty: Roberts, Moraes, and Ferguson, "Geoeconomics." On cyber security governance: Michael Connell and Sarah Vogler, *Russia's Approach to Cyber Warfare* (Washington, DC: Center for Naval Analysis, 2016); Joe Uchill, "More Than 50 Nations, but Not U.S., Sign onto Cybersecurity Pact," *Axios,* November 12, 2018, https://www.axios.com/cybersecurity-paris-call-for-trust-france-21e434df-8a59-48bc-8cde-cd1c1f43dfd0.html. On autonomous weapons: Campaign to Stop Killer Robots, "Convergence on Retaining Human Control of Weapons Systems," Campaign to Stop Killer Robots, April 13, 2018, https://www.stopkillerrobots.org/2018/04/convergence/. On space: Brian Chow, "Space Arms Control: A Hybrid Approach," *Strategic Studies Quarterly* 12, no. 2 (Summer 2018): 107–32.

14. On CSTO: Paul Stronski and Richard Sokolsky, *The Return of Global Russia: An Analytical Framework* (Washington, DC: Carnegie Endowment for International Peace, 2017), 9; Paul Stronski and Nicole Ng, *Cooperation and Competition: Russia and China in Central Asia, the Russian Far East, and the Arctic* (Washington, DC: Carnegie Endowment for International Peace, 2018); "Armenia Contradicts Kremlin on Postponement of CSTO Summit," *Radio Free Liberty Europe/Radio Library's Armenian Service,* December 5, 2018; Catherine Putz, "Who Postponed the CSTO Summit?" *Diplomat,* December 6, 2018, https://thediplomat.com/2018/12/who-postponed-the-csto-summit/. On EAEU: Rilka Dragneva and Kataryn Wolczuk, *The Eurasian Economic Union: Deals, Rules and the Exercise of Power* (London: Chatham House, 2017); "Eurasian Economic Union: Recent Trends and Prospects," Valdai Discussion Club event summary, June 26, 2017, http://valdaiclub.com/events/own/eurasian-economic-union-recent-trends-and-prospects-economic-seminar-/; Radin and Reach, *Russian Views of the International Order,* 57.

15. Austin Long, "Red Glare: The Origin and Implications of Russia's New Nuclear Weapons," *War on the Rocks,* March 26, 2018, https://warontherocks.com/2018/03/red-glare-the-origin-and-implications-of-russias-new-nuclear-weapons/; Radin and Reach, *Russian Views of the International Order,* 59; Robbie Gramer and Lara Seligman, "The INF Treaty Is Dead. Is New START Next?" *Foreign Policy,* February 1, 2019.

16. Dimitri Trenin, "Looking out Five Years: What Should Washington and Its European Allies Expect from Moscow?" Carnegie Moscow Center, August 24, 2017, https://carnegie.ru/commentary/72813.

17. Stewart Patrick and Preeti Bhattacharji, "Rising India: Implications for World Order and International Institutions," Council on Foreign Relations meeting note, November 2010, https://www.cfr.org/content/thinktank/IIGG_Del

himeetingNote_2010_11_01.pdf; Deepa M. Ollapally, "India and the International Order: Accommodation and Adjustment," *Ethics & International Affairs* 32, no. 1 (2018): 65; Waheguru Pal Sing Sidhu, Pratap Bhanu Mehta, and Bruce D. Jones, eds., *Shaping the Emerging World: India and the Multilateral Order* (Washington, DC: Brookings Institution Press, 2013); Paul Staniland, "India's New Security Order," *War on the Rocks*, December 17, 2019, https://warontherocks.com/2019/12/indias-new-security-order/; Dexter Filkins, "Has Narendra Modi Finally Gone Too Far?" *New Yorker*, December 16, 2019, https://www.newyorker.com/news/daily-comment/has-narendra-modi-finally-gone-too-far-india-protests.

18. Mark Hibbs, *Eyes on the Prize: India's Pursuit of Membership in the Nuclear Suppliers Group* (Washington, DC: Carnegie Endowment for International Peace, 2018), 70; Patrick and Bhattacharji, "Rising India," 3; Rajan Menon, "India's Tough Road to the Security Council," *National Interest*, April 4, 2013; Jayita Sarkar and Sumit Ganguly, "India and the NPT After 50 Years," *Diplomat*, June 22, 2018, https://thediplomat.com/2018/06/india-and-the-npt-after-50-years/.

19. Ollapally, "India and the International Order," 64, 67–68; Neelam Deo, "India Has a Unique Opportunity to Shape the Emerging Global Order," *Quartz India*, July 17, 2018; Kirtika Suneja, "WTO Reforms: India Readies Counter to US, Set to Float Paper That Could Stir the Davos Pot," *Economic Times*, January 24, 2019; "India Urges IMF to Implement Quota Reforms," *Economic Times*, October 14, 2018; Nick Buxton and Nicola Bullard, eds., *Shifting Power: Critical Perspectives on Emerging Economies* (Amsterdam: Transnational Institute, 2014), 67–68; Brenda Goh, "BRICS Development Bank to Expand Lending to Private Sector," Reuters, May 29, 2018, https://www.reuters.com/article/us-china-brics-bank/brics-development-bank-to-expand-lending-to-private-sector-idUSKCN1IU0P2.

20. Chinmayi Arun and Sarvjeet Singh, "Yes to Multi-Stakeholderism," *Hindu*, July 20, 2015; Samir Saran, "Democratic, Innovative and Secure: How India Can Shape the Future of the Internet," World Economic Forum, December 12, 2017, https://www.weforum.org/agenda/2017/12/democratic-innovative-and-secure-how-india-is-vying-for-online-leadership; Vindu Goel, "India Proposes Chinese-Style Internet Censorship," *New York Times*, February 14, 2019; Dhruva Jaishankar, *Internet Freedom 2.1: Lessons from Asia's Development* (Washington, DC: German Marshall Fund, 2015), 15–16; Jeffrey Gettleman, Vindu Goel, and Maria Abi-Habib, "India Adopts the Tactic of Authoritarians: Shutting Down the Internet," *New York Times*, December 17, 2019, https://www.nytimes.com/2019/12/17/world/asia/india-internet-modi-protests.html.

21. Patrick and Bhattacharji, "Rising India," 6; Bihar Patna, "Wasting Time—India's Demographic Challenge," *Economist*, May 11, 2013; Abhijnan Rej, "Beyond India's Quest for a Neoliberal Order," *Washington Quarterly* 40, no. 2 (2017): 145–61; Manoj Kumar, "As 'Foreign' Economic Advisers Leave, a Pro-

tectionist India Returns," Reuters, July 12, 2018, https://www.reuters.com/article/us-india-politics-economists-insight/as-foreign-economic-advisers-leave-a-protectionist-india-returns-idUSKBN1K20UB.

22. Rahul Roy-Chaudhury, "Modi Spells out Free, Open, Inclusive Indo-Pacific Policy," IISS, August 2018, https://www.iiss.org/blogs/analysis/2018/08/modi-free-open-inclusive; "Prime Minister's Keynote Address at Shangri La Dialogue," Ministry of External Affairs, Government of India, June 1, 2018, https://www.mea.gov.in/Speeches-Statements.htm?dtl/29943/Prime+Ministers+Keynote+Address+at+Shangri+La+Dialogue+June+01+2018; Ashley J. Tellis and Sean Mirski, *Crux of Asia: China, India, and the Emerging Global Order* (Washington, DC: Carnegie Endowment for International Peace, 2013); Ollapally, "India and the International Order," 69; Dhruva Jaishankar, *Actualising East: India in a Multipolar Asia* (Singapore: Institute of South Asian Studies/National University of Singapore, 2017), 1–2; Constantino Xavier, "India's 'Like-minded' Partnerships to Counter China in South Asia," Carnegie India, September 11, 2017, https://carnegieindia.org/2017/09/11/india-s-like-minded-partnerships-to-counter-china-in-south-asia-pub-73079.

23. "Official Spokesperson's Response to a Query on Participation of India in OBOR/BRI Forum," Government of India Ministry of External Affairs, May 13, 2017, https://mea.gov.in/media-briefings.htm?dtl/28463/Official+Spokesperson+s+response+to+a+query+on+participation+of+India+in+OBORBRI+Forum.

24. Sheila Smith, *Intimate Rivals* (New York: Columbia University Press, 2015), 21.

25. United Nations Secretariat, "Assessment of Member States' Contributions to the United Nations Regular Budget for the year 2019," December 24, 2018, https://undocs.org/en/ST/ADM/SER.B/992.

26. On the UN: Jeffrey W. Hornung, "The Fate of the World Order Rests on Tokyo's Shoulders," *Foreign Policy*, October 30, 2018; "Japan to Sink to Third-Largest Contributor to U.N. as China Rises," *Japan Times*, December 23, 2018; Hitoshi Chiba, "Promoting Ocean Policy," Public Relations Office, Government of Japan, April 2018, https://www.gov-online.go.jp/eng/publicity/book/hlj/html/201804/201804_01_en.html; Masatsune Katsuno, *Japan's Quest for a Permanent Seat on the United Nations Security Council* (Berlin: Friedrich Ebert Stiftung, 2012); Peter Nadin, "United Nations Security Council Reform," United Nations University, May 1, 2014, https://ourworld.unu.edu/en/united-nations-security-council-reform. On the WTO: Takashi Tsuji, "US, Europe and Japan Push for Stronger WTO Enforcement," *Nikkei Asian Review*, September 18, 2018, https://asia.nikkei.com/Politics/International-Relations/US-Europe-and-Japan-push-for-stronger-WTO-enforcement; Leika Kihara, "Davos: Japan's Abe to Put Trade, Climate at Top of G20 To-do List," Reuters, January 23, 2019, https://www.reuters.com/article/us-davos-meeting-japan/japans-abe-to-put-trade-climate-at-top-of-g20-to-do-list-idUSKCN1PH12O.

27. "Joint Press Statement for the U.S.-Japan Policy Cooperation Dialogue on the Internet Economy," September 17, 2014, http://www.soumu.go.jp/main_content/000314312.pdf; "Freedom on the Net 2017: Japan," Freedom House, https://freedomhouse.org/report/freedom-net/2017/japan; Michihiro Nishi, "Data Protection in Japan to Align with GDPR," Skadden Insights, September 24, 2018, https://www.skadden.com/insights/publications/2018/09/quarterly-insights/data-protection-in-japan-to-align-with-gdpr; "Japan's Cyber Diplomacy," Ministry of Foreign Affairs, Government of Japan, https://www.mofa.go.jp/files/000412327.pdf; Ministry of Foreign Affairs of Japan, "Chapter 3: Japan's Foreign Policy to Promote National and Worldwide Interests," Diplomatic Bluebook 2014, https://www.mofa.go.jp/policy/other/bluebook/2014/html/chapter3/efforts.html.

28. Ministry of Foreign Affairs of Japan, "Chapter 3"; Takako Hikotani, "Trump's Gift to Japan: Time for Tokyo to Invest in the Liberal Order," *Foreign Affairs* 96, no. 5 (September/October 2017): 21–27.

29. Michael J. Green, "Japan's Free and Open Indo-Pacific Strategy as Grand Strategy," Japan Ministry of Foreign Affairs, 2018, https://www.japan.go.jp/tomodachi/_userdata/pdf/2018/spring2018/28_29.pdf; Walter Sim, "Japan Vows Quality Infrastructure in Mekong Region in Push for Free and Open Indo-Pacific," *Straits Times*, October 9, 2018; Purnendra Jain, "Japanese Foreign Aid: What's in It for Japan?" East Asia Forum, July 21, 2016, http://www.eastasiaforum.org/2016/07/21/japanese-foreign-aid-whats-in-it-for-japan; Ralph Jennings, "China vs. Japan on Giving Foreign Aid: 3 Things Other Countries Should Know," *Forbes*, January 15, 2017.

30. Jeffrey W. Hornung, "The Fate of the World Order Rests on Tokyo's Shoulders," *Foreign Policy*, October 30, 2018; Mireya Solis and Jennifer Mason, "As the TPP Lives on, the US Abdicates Trade Leadership," Brookings Institution, March 9, 2018, https://www.brookings.edu/blog/order-from-chaos/2018/03/09/as-the-tpp-lives-on-the-u-s-abdicates-trade-leadership; Agence France-Presse, "Australia Leads Fight to Save Trans-Pacific Partnership Trade Pact," *Guardian*, May 21, 2017; Kaori Kaneko and Takashi Umekawa, "Trans-Pacific Trade Pact, without U.S., to Be Signed in March: Japan," Reuters, January 23, 2018, https://www.reuters.com/article/us-trade-tpp-japan/trans-pacific-trade-pact-without-u-s-to-be-signed-in-march-japan-id-USKBN1FC0X3; Terada Takashi, "How and Why Japan Has Saved the TPP: From Trump Tower to Davos," *Asan Forum* 7, no. 6, February 19, 2018, http://www.theasanforum.org/how-and-why-japan-has-saved-the-tpp-from-trump-tower-to-davos/.

31. Government of Japan, "National Security Strategy," December 17, 2013, 5, http://japan.kantei.go.jp/96_abe/documents/2013/__icsFiles/afieldfile/2013/12/17/NSS.pdf; Adam P. Liff, "Japan's Security Policy in the 'Abe Era': Radical Transformation or Evolutionary Shift?" *Texas National Security Review* 1, no. 3 (May 2018): 8–34; Catharin Dalpino, "Japan-Southeast Asia

Relations: Both Push and Pull; Japan Steps Up in Southeast Asia," *Comparative Connections* 19, no. 1 (May 2017): 123–30; "India-Japan Ties: Asia's Fastest Growing Relationship," Wilson Center Event, November 15, 2011, https:// www.wilsoncenter.org/event/india-japan-ties-asias-fastest-growing-relationship; Mercy A. Kuo, "Japan-US Relations: Indo-Pacific Strategy and the Quad," *Diplomat*, August 8, 2018, https://thediplomat.com/2018/08/japan-us-relations-indo-pacific-strategy-and-the-quad/; Yuki Tatsumi, "Is Japan Ready for the Quad? Opportunities and Challenges for Tokyo in a Changing Indo-Pacific," *War on the Rocks*, January 9, 2018, https://warontherocks.com/2018/01/japan-ready-quad-opportunities-challenges-tokyo-changing-indo-pacific/.

32. Julianne Smith, "German Foreign Policy Is Stuck in Neutral," *War on the Rocks*, February 18, 2019, https://warontherocks.com/2019/02/german-foreign-policy-is-stuck-in-neutral/.

33. Thorsten Benner, "Germany Can Protect the Liberal Order," *Foreign Affairs*, November 16, 2016, https://www.foreignaffairs.com/articles/germany/2016-11 -16/germany-can-protect-liberal-order; Jonas Wolff, "Democracy Promotion and Civilian Power: The Example of Germany's 'Value-Oriented' Foreign Policy," *German Politics* 22, no. 4 (2013): 4. On the UN: German Federal Foreign Office, "Germany in the United Nations," July 20, 2018, https://www.auswaertiges-amt.de/en/aussenpolitik/internationale-organisationen/vereintenationen/-/231548; Markus Kaim and Constanze Stelzenmüller, *New Power, New Responsibility: Elements of a German Foreign and Security Policy for a Changing World* (Berlin: German Marshall Fund, 2013), 17; Nadin, "United Nations Security Council Reform." On the WTO: World Trade Organization, "Joint Communiqué of the Ottawa Ministerial on WTO Reform," October 25, 2018, https:// www.wto.org/english/news_e/news18_e/dgra_26oct18_e.pdf; Charles Akande, "Ministers Brainstorm WTO Reform in Ottawa," *Geneva Watch* 18, no. 26, October 29, 2018, http://chep-poic.ca/wp-content/uploads/2018/11/EN_Geneva_Watch_October_29_2018.pdf; "WTO Reform: EU Proposes Way Forward on the Functioning of the Appellate Body," European Commission, November 25, 2018, http://europa.eu/rapid/press-release_IP-18-6529_en.htm.

34. On climate: German Federal Ministry for the Environment, Nature Conservation and Nuclear Safety, "New Partnership Aims to Help Developing Countries Implement the Paris Agreement," July 4, 2016, https://www.bmu.de/en/pressrelease/new-partnership-aims-to-help-developing-countries-implement-the-paris-agreement-1/. On technology: Constanze Stelzenmüller, "Germany: Between Power and Responsibility," in *Shaper Nations: Strategies for a Changing World*, ed. William Hitchcock, Melvyn Leffler, and Jeffrey Legro (Cambridge, MA: Harvard University Press, 2016), 57; Lennart Schüßler and Natallia Karniyevich, "Germany Is the First EU Member State to Enact New Data Protection Act to Align with the GDPR," *Bird & Bird*, July 2017, https://www.twobirds.com/en/news/articles/2017/germany/germany-is-the-first-eu -member-state-to-enact-new-data-protection-act-to-align-with-the-gdpr;

Nick Wallace and Daniel Castro, *The Impact of the EU's New Data Protection Regulation on AI* (Washington, DC: Center for Data Innovation, 2018), 37; Helen Dixon, "Regulate to Liberate: Can Europe Save the Internet?" *Foreign Affairs* 97, no. 5 (September/October 2018): 28–32; "GDPR: US News Sites Unavailable to EU Users under New Rules," *BBC*, May 25, 2018; George Selfo, "Marketers and Tech Companies Confront California's Version of GDPR," *Ad Age*, June 29, 2018. On the prospect of a splinternet: "There May Soon Be Three Internets. America's Won't Necessarily Be the Best," *New York Times*, October 15, 2018.

35. German Federal Government, "Speech by Federal Chancellor Angela Merkel at the World Economic Forum Annual Meeting in Davos on 24 January 2018," January 24, 2018, https://www.bundesregierung.de/breg-en/chancellor/speech-by-federal-chancellor-angela-merkel-at-the-world-economic-forum-annual-meeting-in-davos-on-24-january-2018–455144; Kaim and Stelzenmüller, *New Power, New Responsibility*, 23; Constanze Stelzenmüller, *Normal Is Over* (Washington, DC: Brookings Institution Press, 2018), 8; German Federal Government, "White Paper on German Security Policy and the Future of the Bundeswehr," July 13, 2016, 6, https://issat.dcaf.ch/download/111704/2027268/2016%20White%20Paper.pdf; Matthias Gebauer, "Germany Remains Tepid on NATO 2-Percent Goal," *Der Spiegel Online*, November 7, 2019; Lewis Sanders IV, "How Does Germany Contribute to NATO?" *DW*, March 9, 2018.

36. On EU unity: Ishaan Tharoor, "Europe's Constant Struggle with Enemies Abroad and Within," *Washington Post*, September 6, 2018. On Germany's strategic relationship to the EU: Thomas Bagger, "The World According to Germany: Reassessing 1989," *Washington Quarterly* 41, no. 4 (2019): 53–63.

FIVE

Toward an Open World

1. Michael J. Green, *By More Than Providence: Grand Strategy and American Power in the Asia-Pacific* (New York: Columbia University Press, 2017); Hal Brands and Charles Edel, "The Disharmony of the Spheres," *Commentary*, December 2017.

2. Stewart M. Patrick, "America's Quest for an Open World: A Grand Strategy Grounded in History," *World Politics Review*, April 29, 2019.

3. Eduard Mark, "American Policy toward Eastern Europe and the Origins of the Cold War, 1941–1946: An Alternative Interpretation," *Journal of American History* 68, no. 2 (September 1981): 313–36; Colin Dueck, "Realism, Culture, and Grand Strategy: Explaining America's Peculiar Path to World Power," *Security Studies* 14, no. 2 (2005): 195–231; Walter Lippmann, *U.S. Foreign Policy: Shield of the Republic* (Boston: Little, Brown, 1943).

4. Dueck, "Realism, Culture, and Grand Strategy"; Patrick, "America's Quest for an Open World."

5. Kurt M. Campbell and Jake Sullivan, "Competition without Catastrophe: How America Can Both Challenge and Coexist with China," *Foreign Affairs* 98, no. 5 (September/October 2019): 96–111; Stephen Brooks, *Producing Security: Multinational Corporations, Globalization, and the Changing Calculus of Conflict* (Princeton: Princeton University Press, 2005). The literature offering "long peace" explanations is voluminous, and the arguments themselves are not mutually exclusive. A sample of seminal works include Kenneth N. Waltz, *Theory of International Politics* (Reading, MA: Addison-Wesley, 1979), 180–81; Kenneth N. Waltz, "The Spread of Nuclear Weapons: More May Be Better," in *Adelphi Papers* 21 (London: International Institute for Strategic Studies, 1981); Richard Rosecrance et al., "Whither Interdependence?" *International Organization* 31, no. 3 (1977): 425; Richard Rosecrance, *The Rise of the Trading State: Commerce and Conquest in the Modern World* (New York: Basic Books, 1986); Zeev Maoz and Bruce Russett, "Normative and Structural Causes of the Democratic Peace, 1946–1986," *American Political Science Review* 87, no. 3 (1993): 624–38; Alexander Wendt, *Social Theory of International Politics* (New York: Cambridge University Press, 1999); Mark W. Zacher, "The Territorial Integrity Norm: International Boundaries and the Use of Force," *International Organization* 55, no. 2 (Spring 2001): 215–50; Robert L. Jervis, "Theories of War in an Era of Leading Power Peace: Presidential Address, American Political Science Association, 2001," *American Political Science Review* 96, no. 1 (March 2002): 1–14.
6. Jennifer Lind, "Life in China's Asia," *Foreign Affairs* 97, no. 2 (March/April 2018): 71–82. On imperial structures: Daniel H. Nexon and Thomas Wright, "What's at Stake in the American Empire Debate," *American Political Science Review* 101, no. 2 (2007): 253–71.
7. For a modern-day sphere of influence strategy, see Peter Beinart, "America Needs an Entirely New Foreign Policy for the Trump Age," *Atlantic*, September 16, 2018.
8. Mira Rapp-Hooper, "All in Good FON: Why Freedom of Navigation Is Business as Usual in the South China Sea," *Foreign Affairs*, October 12, 2015, https://www.foreignaffairs.com/articles/united-states/2015-10-12/all-good-fon.
9. Hal Brands and Eric Edelman, *Avoiding a Strategy of Bluff: The Crisis of American Military Primacy* (Washington, DC: Center for Strategic and Budgetary Assessments, 2017).
10. Barry Posen, *Restraint: A New Foundation for U.S. Grand Strategy* (Ithaca: Cornell University Press, 2014); Stephen M. Walt, *The Hell of Good Intentions: America's Foreign Policy Elite and the Decline of U.S. Primacy* (New York: Farrar, Straus and Giroux, 2018).
11. Alastair Iain Johnston, "The Failures of the 'Failure of Engagement' with China," *Washington Quarterly* 42, no. 2 (Summer 2019).
12. Thomas Wright, "The Return to Great Power Rivalry Was Inevitable," *Atlantic*, September 12, 2018.

13. For the most comprehensive treatment of China's foreign policy objectives under Xi Jinping, see Elizabeth C. Economy, *The Third Revolution: Xi Jinping and the New Chinese State* (New York: Oxford University Press, 2018). See also Zheng Wang, "The Chinese Dream: Concept and Context," *Journal of Chinese Political Science* 19, no. 1, December 13, 2013, https://www7.shu.edu/diplomacy/upload/The-Chinese-Dream-Concept-and-Context-JCPS-Zheng-Wang.pdf; Christopher K. Johnson, *Decoding China's Emerging 'Great Power' Strategy in Asia* (Washington, DC: CSIS, 2014); Andrew Nathan and Andrew Scobell, "How China Sees America: The Sum of Beijing's Fears," *Foreign Affairs* 91, no. 5 (September/October 2012): 32–47; Rush Doshi, "Xi Jinping Just Made It Clear Where China's Foreign Policy Is Headed," *Washington Post*, October 25, 2017; Graham Allison, "What Xi Jinping Wants," *Atlantic*, May 31, 2017.

14. Carl Minzer, *End of an Era: How China's Authoritarian Revival Is Undermining Its Rise* (New York: Oxford University Press, 2018); Adrian Shahbaz, *Freedom on the Net, 2018: The Rise of Digital Authoritarianism* (Washington, DC: Freedom House, 2018).

15. See, e.g., Oriana Skylar Mastro, "The Stealth Superpower: How China Hid Its Global Ambitions," *Foreign Affairs* 98, no. 1 (January/February 2019): 31–39, foreignaffairs.com/articles/china/china-plan-rule-asia; Lind, "Life in China's Asia."

16. Evan Feigenbaum, "Reluctant Stakeholder: Why China's Brand of Revisionism Is More Challenging Than Washington Thinks," *MacroPolo*, April 27, 2018.

17. John Schaus, Michael Matlaga, Kathleen H. Hicks, Heather A. Conley, and Jeff Rathke, "What Works: Countering Grey Zone Coercion," CSIS Brief, July 16, 2018, https://www.csis.org/analysis/what-works-countering-gray-zone-coercion; Kathleen H. Hicks and Alice Hunt Friend, *By Other Means: Part I—Campaigning in the Grey Zone* (Washington, DC: CSIS, July 2019).

18. Tom Wheeler and Robert D. Williams, "Keeping Huawei out of the U.S. Is Not Enough to Secure 5G," *Lawfare*, February 20, 2019, https://www.lawfareblog.com/keeping-huawei-hardware-out-us-not-enough-secure-5g.

19. For this "early-warning" framing we are grateful to the participants of our July 2019 "Grand Strategic Futures" exercise in Newport, Rhode Island, at the Naval War College.

20. Jon Temin and Daniel Summers, "Democratic Governance in Africa: Three Key Trends," Freedom House, May 10, 2018, https://freedomhouse.org/blog/democratic-governance-africa-three-key-trends.

21. Matthias Sobolewski and Jason Lange, "US Urges Allies to Think Twice Before Joining China-Led Bank," Reuters, March 16, 2015, https://www.reuters.com/article/us-europe-asia-bank/u-s-urges-allies-to-think-twice-before-joining-china-led-bank-idUSKBN0MD0B320150317; Sabrina Snell, "US Allies Split with Washington, Bank with China," U.S.-China Economic and Security Review Commission, Issue Brief, March 31, 2015, https://www.uscc.gov/sites/

default/files/Research/Asian%20Infrastructure%20Investment%20Bank_
Issue%20Brief.pdf.

22. Carl Thayer, "South China Sea: A Commons for China Only?" *Yale Global Online*, July 7, 2011; U.S. Department of Defense, "Asia-Pacific Maritime Security Strategy," August 21, 2015, https://dod.defense.gov/Portals/1/Documents/pubs/NDAA%20A-P_Maritime_SecuritY_Strategy-08142015-1300-FINAL-FORMAT.PDF.

23. Rebecca Friedman Lissner and Mira Rapp-Hooper, "The Liberal Order Is More Than a Myth," *Foreign Affairs*, July 31, 2018, https://www.foreignaffairs.com/articles/world/2018-07-31/liberal-order-more-myth; Johnston, "The Failures of the 'Failures of Engagement' with China."

24. Dina Smeltz et al., *Rejecting Retreat: Americans Support U.S. Engagement in Global Affairs* (Chicago: Chicago Council on Global Affairs, 2019); Laura Silver, Kat Devlin, and Christine Huang, "U.S. Views of China Turn Sharply Negative amidst Trade Tensions," Pew Research Center, Global Attitudes and Trends, August 13, 2019, https://www.pewresearch.org/global/2019/08/13/u-s-views-of-china-turn-sharply-negative-amid-trade-tensions/.

SIX

A Policy for the Day After

1. On immigration: Donald Kerwin, *Moving beyond Comprehensive Immigration Reform and Trump: Principles, Interests, and Policies to Guide Long-Term Reform of the US Immigration System* (Washington, DC: Center for Migration Studies, 2017). On education: Lisette Partelow et al., *Fixing Chronic Disinvestment in K-12 Schools* (Washington, DC: Center for American Progress, 2018); Richard Haass, *Foreign Policy Begins at Home* (New York: Basic Books, 2013), 136–37; Michael O'Hanlon, "America's Place in the World Depends on Conditions at Home (and the Middle Class)," Brookings Institution, November 15, 2018, https://www.brookings.edu/opinions/americas-place-in-the-world-depends-on-conditions-at-home-and-the-middle-class.

2. We are grateful to Jared Cohen for his suggestions for new tech talent programs. See also Amy Zegart and Kevin Childs, "The Divide between Silicon Valley and Washington Is a National-Security Threat," *Atlantic*, December 13, 2018.

3. James Manyika, William H. McRaven, and Adam Segal, "Innovation and National Security: Keeping Our Edge," Independent Task Force Report no. 77, Council on Foreign Relations, 2019, 31, https://www.cfr.org/report/keeping-our-edge/pdf/TFR_Innovation_Strategy.pdf; Senate Committee on the Judiciary, *Hearing on 5G: The Impact on National Security, Intellectual Property, and Competition*, May 14, 2019, statement of Dr. Charles Clancy, Bradley Professor of Cybersecurity, Virginia Tech, 32, https://www.judiciary.senate.gov/imo/media/doc/Clancy%20Testimony.pdf.

183

4. J. Michael McQuade et al., *Software Is Never Done: Refactoring the Acquisition Code for Competitive Advantage* (Washington, DC: Defense Innovation Board, 2019); Manyika, McRaven, and Segal, "Innovation and National Security," 17, 38; Eric Schmidt et al., "Interim Report of the National Security Commission on Artificial Intelligence," National Security Commission on Artificial Intelligence, November 2019, 30–33, https://www.epic.org/foia/epic-v-ai-commission/AI-Commission-Interim-Report-Nov-2019.pdf. For an example of a fast-tracked contracting process, see "$40M Available for Start-ups, Small Businesses through Air Force Pitch Day," Air Force Material Command, January 15, 2019, https://www.afmc.af.mil/News/Article-Display/Article/1732301/40m-available-for-start-ups-small-businesses-through-air-force-pitch-day/.

5. On a NETC: Julian Baird Gewirtz, "China's Long March to Technological Supremacy," *Foreign Affairs*, August 27, 2019. We are grateful to Jared Cohen for suggesting a National Security Strategy tech annex.

6. Zachary K. Goldman, "Sanctioning Cyber Crime: The New Face of Deterrence," Council on Foreign Relations, May 19, 2015, https://www.cfr.org/blog/sanctioning-cyber-crime-new-face-deterrence.

7. Jared Cohen, "The US, China, and the Future of the Splinternet" (working paper, Aspen Strategy Group, August 2019).

8. Peter Trubowitz and Nichole Mellow, "Foreign Policy, Bipartisanship, and the Paradox of Post–September 11 America," *International Politics* 48, nos. 2/3 (2011): 164–87.

9. On public service: National Commission on Military, National, and Public Service, *Interim Report*, January 2019, https://www.inspire2serve.gov/reports/interim. On public opinion about great-power competition: Richard Fontaine, "Great-Power Competition Is Washington's Top Priority—but not the Public's," *Foreign Affairs*, September 9, 2019, https://www.foreignaffairs.com/articles/china/2019-09-09/great-power-competition-washingtons-top-priority-not-publics.

10. On State Department funding: "Strike Three: Once Again International Affairs Programs Slashed, out of Step with Today's Global Realities," U.S. Global Leadership Coalition, March 11, 2019, https://www.usglc.org/media/2019/03/USGLC-FY20-Budget-Analysis.pdf. On gray zone diplomacy: Caleb D. Becker, "Are U.S. Diplomats Ready for War?" *War on the Rocks*, July 1, 2019, https://warontherocks.com/2019/07/are-u-s-diplomats-ready-for-war/. On foreign service recruitment: Elizabeth Warren, "Revitalizing Diplomacy: A 21st Century Foreign Service," *Medium*, June 28, 2019, https://medium.com/@teamwarren/revitalizing-diplomacy-a-21st-century-foreign-service-2d9d195698f; Kori N. Schake and Brett McGurk, "Compete with China? Support a GI Bill for Diplomacy," *Washington Post*, May 13, 2019.

11. For an explication of a similar standard of "military sufficiency," see Van Jackson, "Wagering on a Progressive versus Liberal Theory of National Security," Policy Roundtable: The Future of Progressive Foreign Policy, *Texas National*

Security Review, December 4, 2018, https://tnsr.org/roundtable/policy-round-table-the-future-of-progressive-foreign-policy/.

12. For this framing we are grateful to the participants of our July 2019 "Grand Strategic Futures" exercise.

13. On force planning: Mark Gunzinger et al., *Force Planning in the Era of Great Power Competition* (Washington, DC: Center for Strategic and Budgetary Assessments, 2017); Todd Harrison, *Outside Perspectives on Military Personnel Policy, before the House of Representatives Subcommittee on Military Personnel,* 116th Cong. (2019), https://csis-prod.s3.amazonaws.com/s3fs-public/congressional_testimony/ts090312_Harrison.pdf; Todd Harrison and Seamus P. Daniels, *Analysis of the FY 2019 Defense Budget* (Washington, DC: Center for Strategic and International Studies, 2018). On the audit: Idrees Ali and Mike Stone, "Pentagon Fails Its First-Ever Audit, Official Says," Reuters, November 15, 2018, https://www.reuters.com/article/us-usa-pentagon-audit/pentagon-fails-its-first-ever-audit-official-says-idUSKCN1NK2MC.

14. Michael O'Hanlon, *The Senkaku Paradox: Risking Great Power War over Small States* (Washington, DC: Brookings Institution Press, 2019), chapter 1; Michael J. Green, Kathleen H. Hicks, John Schaus, Zack Cooper, and Jake Douglas, *Countering Coercion in Maritime Asia: The Theory and Practice of Gray Zone Deterrence* (Washington, DC: Center for Strategic and International Studies, 2017), https://www.csis.org/analysis/countering-coercion-maritime-asia; Lyle J. Morris et al., *Gaining Competitive Advantage in the Gray Zone* (Santa Monica: RAND, 2019).

15. Jessica Brandt and Joshua Rudolf, "A New National Security Framework for Foreign Interference," *Just Security,* September 27, 2019, https://www.justsecurity.org/66357/a-new-national-security-framework-for-foreign-interference/.

16. Eric Edelman et al., *Providing for the Common Defense: The Assessment and Recommendations of the National Defense Strategy Commission* (Washington, DC: United States Institute of Peace, 2018), 9.

17. We are grateful to Michèle Flournoy and Kath Hicks for highlighting the importance of commercial tools. On artificial intelligence: Office of the Director of National Intelligence, "The AIM Initiative: A Strategy for Augmenting Intelligence Using Machines," January 2019, https://www.dni.gov/files/ODNI/documents/AIM-Strategy.pdf. On the gray zone: Lindsey R. Sheppard, "Warning for the Gray Zone," Center for Strategic and International Studies, August 13, 2019, https://www.csis.org/analysis/warning-gray-zone; Defense Science Board, "Summer Study on Capabilities for Constrained Military Operations," December 2016, https://dsb.cto.mil/reports/2010s/DSBSS16_CMO.pdf.

18. Charlene Barshefsky et al., "The Higher Road: Forging a US Strategy for the Global Infrastructure Challenge," Center for Strategic and International Studies, April 2019, 4–5, https://csis-prod.s3.amazonaws.com/s3fs-public/

publication/190423_Hadley%20et%20al_HigherRoads_report_WEB.pdf?yh JKzmr9nDmurxGM3H5iivvQgVeXchpR.

19. Ben Kesling and Jon Emont, "U.S. Goes on the Offensive against China's Empire-Building Funding Plan, *Wall Street Journal*, April 9, 2017; Barshefsky et al., "The Higher Road," 3–4.

20. For GDP figures: United States Department of Agriculture, "International Macroeconomic Data Set," August 20, 2019, https://www.ers.usda.gov/data-products/international-macroeconomic-data-set/.

21. Mira Rapp-Hooper, *Shields of the Republic: Triumph and Peril in America's Alliances* (Cambridge, MA: Harvard University Press, 2019), chapters 1–3.

22. Rapp-Hooper, *Shields of the Republic*, chapter 7; Cohen, "The US, China, and the Future of the Splinternet."

23. Celeste A. Wallander, "NATO's Enemies Within: How Democratic Decline Could Destroy the Alliance," *Foreign Affairs* 97, no. 4 (July/August 2018): 70–81.

24. We are grateful to Jared Cohen for suggesting a pooled 5G network. On a similar approach to AI: Schmidt et al., "Interim Report of the National Security Commission on Artificial Intelligence," 45.

25. Aaron Friedberg, *Beyond Air-Sea Battle: The Debate over US Military Strategy in Asia* (London: International Institute for Strategic Studies, 2014); Thomas G. Mahnken, "Weapons: The Growth & Spread of the Precision-Strike Regime," *Daedalus* 140, no. 3 (Summer 2011): 45–57; Evan B. Montgomery, "Contested Primacy in the Western Pacific: China's Rise and the Future of US Power Projection," *International Security* 38, no. 4 (2014): 115–49; Eric Sayers, "Assessing America's Indo-Pacific Budget Shortfall," *War on the Rocks*, November 15, 2018, https://warontherocks.com/2018/11/assessing-americas-indo-pacific-budget-shortfall/.

26. We are grateful to Tamara Wittes for suggesting integrated anti-piracy coalitions in these regions. See also Neil Melvin, *The Foreign Military Presence in the Horn of Africa Region*, SIPRI Background Paper, April 2019, https://www.sipri.org/sites/default/files/2019-05/sipribp1904_2.pdf; Farzin Nadimi, "Clarifying Freedom of Navigation in the Gulf," Washington Institute, July 24, 2019, https://www.washingtoninstitute.org/policy-analysis/view/clarifying-freedom-of-navigation-in-the-gulf.

27. Stewart Patrick and Kyle Evanoff, "The Right Way to Achieve Security in Space," *Foreign Affairs*, September 17, 2018, https://www.foreignaffairs.com/articles/space/2018-09-17/right-way-achieve-security-space; Joan Johnson-Freese and David Burbach, "The Outer Space Treaty and the Weaponization of Space," *Bulletin of the Atomic Scientists* 75, no. 4 (2019): 137–41; James Clay Moltz, *Crowded Orbits: Conflict and Cooperation in Space* (New York: Columbia University Press, 2014); Frank A. Rose, "America in Space: Future Visions, Current Issues," Brookings Institution, March 14, 2019, https://www.brookings.edu/testimonies/america-in-space-future-visions-current-issues; Frank A.

Rose, "Safeguarding the Heavens: The United States and the Future of Norms of Behavior in Outer Space," Brookings Institution, June 2018, https://www.brookings.edu/wp-content/uploads/2018/06/FP_20180614_safeguarding_the_heavens.pdf.

28. Jennifer Hillman, "Three Approaches to Fixing the World Trade Organization's Appellate Body: The Good, the Bad and the Ugly?" Institute of International Economic Law, Georgetown University Law Center, December 2018, https://www.law.georgetown.edu/wp-content/uploads/2018/12/Hillman-Good-Bad-Ugly-Fix-to-WTO-AB.pdf.

29. On state subsidies: Naoyuki Toyama and Rintaro Hosokawa, "India, US Combine to Stymie WTO Ministerial Meeting," *Nikkei Asian Review*, December 14, 2017; United Nations Conference on Trade and Development, "Key Statistics and Trends in Trade Policy: 2018," United Nations, 2019, 19, https://unctad.org/en/PublicationsLibrary/ditctab2019d1_en.pdf. On an SOE code of conduct and a related U.S.-EU-Japan proposal: Gary Hufbauer et al., "From Drift to Deals: Advancing the WTO Agenda," Peterson Institute for International Economics, June 2015, 49–51, 62, https://www.piie.com/publications/papers/hufbauer-etal201506ICC.pdf; Jack Caporal, "U.S.-Japan Trade Talks: What Could They Yield?" Center for Strategic and International Studies, September 28, 2018, https://www.csis.org/analysis/us-japan-trade-talks-what-could-they-yield; "Joint Statement, on Trilateral Meeting of the Trade Ministers of the United States, Japan, and the European Union," Office of the U.S. Trade Representative, September 5, 2018, https://ustr.gov/about-us/policy-offices/press-office/press-releases/2018/september/joint-statement-trilateral. On China's compliance record: James Bacchus, Simon Lester, and Huan Zhu, *Disciplining China's Trade Practices at the WTO* (Washington, DC: Cato Institute, 2018).

30. International Monetary Fund, the World Bank, and World Trade Organization, *Reinvigorating Trade and Inclusive Growth* (Washington, DC: World Bank Group, 2018), 9–14; International Centre for Trade and Sustainable Development (ICTSD), "Updating the Multilateral Rule Book on E-Commerce," ICTSD Policy Brief, March 2018, https://www.ictsd.org/sites/default/files/research/electronic_commerce_negotiations-ictsd_policy_brief_2018.pdf; Rachel Fefer, *Trade in Services Agreement (TiSA) Negotiations: Overview and Issues for Congress* (Washington, DC: Congressional Research Service, 2017); Ali Wyne, "Economic Multilateralism and Regionalism," RAND Corporation, January 2018, https://www.rand.org/blog/2018/01/economic-multilateralism-and-regionalism.html.

31. Mark Wu, "The 'China, Inc.' Challenge to Global Trade Governance," *Harvard International Law Journal* 57, no. 2 (Spring 2016): 261–324.

32. Kimberly Clausing, *Open: The Progressive Case for Free Trade, Immigration, and Global Capital* (Cambridge, MA: Harvard University Press, 2019), 92–114.

33. James McBride and Andrew Chatzky, "What Is the Trans-Pacific Partnership (TPP)?" Council on Foreign Relations, January 4, 2019, https://www.cfr.org/

backgrounder/what-trans-pacific-partnership-tpp; Kazuhito Yamashita, "Use the TPP to Reform the WTO!—WTO Reform Is Necessary to Restrict China's Actions," Canon Institute for Global Studies, August 22, 2018, https://www.canon-igs.org/en/column/macroeconomics/20180822_5215.html; Jeffrey J. Schott, "TPP Can Be Fixed if You Know What's Wrong with It," Peterson Institute for International Economics, December 5, 2016, https://piie.com/blogs/trade-investment-policy-watch/tpp-can-be-fixed-if-you-know-whats-wrong-it; Matthew Goodman, "From TPP to CPTPP," Center for Strategic and International Studies, March 8, 2018, https://www.csis.org/analysis/tpp-cptpp.

34. Elaine Korzak, "UN GGE on Cybersecurity: The End of an Era?" *Diplomat*, July 31, 2017, https://thediplomat.com/2017/07/un-gge-on-cybersecurity-have-china-and-russia-just-made-cyberspace-less-safe/.

35. Hilary McGeachy, *US-China Technology Competition: Impacting a Rules-Based Order* (Sydney: United States Studies Center at the University of Sydney, 2019); "Five Things You Need to Know about France's Cyber Norm Proposal," New America, November 13, 2018, https://www.newamerica.org/cybersecurity-initiative/c2b/c2b-log/five-things-you-need-to-know-about-frances-new-cyber-norm-proposal/; Josh Gold, "The First Ever Meeting on Cyber Norms Holds Promise, but Challenges Remain," Council on Foreign Relations, September 20, 2109, https://www.cfr.org/blog/first-global-meeting-cyber-norms?utm_medium=social_share&utm_source=tw.

36. Kanta Kumari Rigaud et al., *Groundswell: Preparing for Internal Climate Migration* (Washington, DC: World Bank Group, 2018).

37. "Joe's Plan for a Clean Energy Revolution and Environmental Justice," Biden for President, https://joebiden.com/Climate/.

38. Kara C. McDonald and Stewart M. Patrick, *UN Security Council Enlargement and U.S. Interests* (New York: Council on Foreign Relations, 2010), 21; Stewart M. Patrick, "Why Is No One Talking about UNSC Reform Anymore?" *World Politics Review*, June 3, 2019.

39. This most closely resembles the Group of Four plan proposed by Japan, India, Germany, and Brazil. Patrick, "Why Is No One Talking about UNSC Reform Anymore?" Also see McDonald and Patrick, *UN Security Council Enlargement and U.S. Interests* for supporting details.

Index

Index

decolonization, 15, 21–22

Defense Department, 33, 121, 125, 133

Defense Innovation Unit (DIU), 32, 125

defense spending: authoritarianism and, 54; in Germany, 84; national debt and, 40–41; private sector and, 32–33, 125; U.S. allies and, 51–52. *See also* militaries; security

democracy: in Africa, 113; alliances supporting, 138; as benefit of liberal order, 22; disinformation and, 41–42; election interference and, 30, 109; liberal order's decline and, 11; openness strategy and, 7, 91, 101, 103, 109, 122, 127; technology in, 55–57, 59–60, 148

Democratic Party, 34–39, 127–30

Department of ___. *See name of department by remaining portion of name*

deterrence: gray zone conflict and, 8, 130–31, 133–34, 149; military sufficiency and, 132–33, 184n11; in openness strategy, 107, 137; private sector and, 126

digital authoritarianism, 4, 45, 54–57, 59–60, 96, 105, 148–49

digital commerce, 145–46

disease and pandemics, 87, 97, 116, 149, 150

disinformation, 41–42, 58, 126, 134

DIU (Defense Innovation Unit), 32, 125

dollar primacy, 41, 44, 49

domestic politics and policies: disinformation and, 41–42; federal spending and, 40–41; financial crisis of 2008 and, 13; foreign policy impacts of, 29–30, 42–43, 59–60, 83, 123, 152; income inequality and, 37–38, 90, 116; international character vs., 90,

103, 105; in openness strategy, 98, 116, 121–23; political polarization in, 34–37; public opinion and, 39–40; technology and, 30–34, 123–27. *See also specific countries*

EAEU (Eurasian Economics Union), 72

early warning, 111, 132, 182n19

economic competitiveness, 8, 51, 90, 126

economic inequality. *See* income inequality

economics and economic power: Asian multipolarity in, 46–47, 52–54, 58–59, 77, 87; China and, 47–48, 81, 84–85; EU and, 85–86; foreign policy and, 29–30; Germany and, 83, 84; gray zone conflict and, 58; India and, 76–77; international influence through, 15–16, 46–47, 49–50; Japan and, 79, 81; liberal international order and, 12, 22–24, 87; in openness strategy, 28, 94, 107–8; Russia and, 48, 72; United States and, 49–50, 57, 81; of U.S. alliance assets, 50–52; war and, 23, 25–26

education and education reform, 38, 123–25

election interference: disinformation and, 41; lack of governance and, 24, 32, 134; openness strategy addressing, 89, 134; polarization and, 30, 42; Russia and, 24, 32, 70, 109, 114, 128; spheres of influence and, 95; Trump and, 114, 128

empire, 17, 95–96, 157n14

energy industry, 66, 71, 124, 129, 150

England. *See* United Kingdom

192

entrepreneurship, institutional, 62–63, 67, 75, 80–82, 140
Eurasian Economics Union (EAEU), 72
European Union (EU): as alliance assets, 50–51; Communist order vs., 20–21; geographic scope of, 15; Germany's role in, 82–85; openness strategy and, 108–10, 119, 132, 137; Russia and, 49, 63, 97; trade reform and, 147; WTO and, 79
EXIM Bank (Export-Import Bank, U.S.), 136
expertise: of media elites, 36; need for government to improve tech workforce, 124; of STEM talent, 32
Export-Import Bank (EXIM, U.S.), 136
exports. *See* trade

Facebook, 32, 126
fellowships and scholarships in technology, 124–25
financial crisis of 2008, 13, 40
First Island Chain defense strategy, 96, 132, 141–42
5G networks, 95, 113, 123, 138–39, 149, 186n24
FOIPS (Free and Open Indo-Pacific Strategy), 80
FON (freedom of navigation), 138, 142
foreign aid: climate governance and, 76; Germany and, 83; Japan and, 80–81; liberal order and, 22; military financing and, 142; in openness strategy, 101, 104
foreign policy: debt and, 40–41; disinformation and, 41–42; domestic politics, effect on, 29–30, 42–43, 59–60, 83, 123, 152; on illiberal/mixed states, 100–103, 115; immigration and, 29–30; income inequality and,

37–38; liberal order's decline and, 11–13; openness strategy for, 113–19, 127–30, 152–53; polarization's impacts on, 4, 30, 34–37, 42–43, 59–60, 120, 123, 127–30; prosperity and, 89–90; public opinion on, 30, 39–40, 118, 130; Trump and, 1–3, 10, 114, 120, 128, 152
France and liberal international order, 17–18
Free and Open Indo-Pacific Strategy (FOIPS), 80
freedom of navigation (FON), 138, 142
free markets: diversity in, 136; Germany and, 84; globalization and, 94; innovation and, 56; Japan and, 81; liberal international order and, 11–12, 20–21, 102; tech sector and, 31–33; TiSA and, 145–46
free trade. *See* trade

G20 (Group of Twenty), 64, 79
GDP (gross domestic product) and power, 46, 47, 49, 51, 109, 186n20
GDPR (General Data Protection Regulation), 79, 83–85
General Agreement on Tariff and Trade (GATT), 22, 92, 145. *See also* World Trade Organization
General Data Protection Regulation (GDPR), 79, 83–85
Geneva Convention (1929), 19
Germany: Concert of Europe and, 18; domestic policies in, 85–86; global strategy of, 82–87; infrastructure investment and, 139; Iran nuclear deal and, 140; Japan and, 79; League of Nations and, 20; as regional steward, 84–85; U.S. strategy and, 28, 88

Index

Korea, 19, 23
Kosovo, 84

labor practices and trade, 146
Latin America, 112–13. *See also specific countries*
League of Nations, 19–20
Lethal Autonomous Weapons Pledge, 33
liberal international order: authoritarian regimes and, 23–24, 58, 64, 87, 102, 118; Cold War and, 93; decline/durability of, 11–13, 25–28, 44, 52, 61, 73, 86–88, 116–17; Germany and, 83; internet governance and, 75–76; Japan and, 79–82; obsolescence of, 3; openness strategy compared to, 90, 101–2, 114–15, 118, 119; post–World War I, 19–20; post–World War II, 20–21; record of, 21–25; Trump and, 1–2; U.S. behavior censured, 16
liberal universalism, 7, 9, 21, 23, 25, 86, 93, 102, 118–19
"long peace" arguments, 23, 181n5

Made in China 2025 plan, 126
maritime rules, 66, 67, 69, 99, 110, 142–43
markets. *See* free markets; nonmarket economies
media polarization of partisan news, 35–36, 41–42
Mexico, 113
Middle East: global commons and, 138, 141–43; military presence in, 132; openness strategy and, 7, 90–91, 103, 110–12, 137. *See also specific countries*
middle powers: alliances with, 59, 60, 137, 139; liberal order's decline and, 5, 25; openness strategy and, 106–7;

State Department and, 131; strength of, 5, 45, 54; TPP and, 81; UNSC representation for, 86
migration. *See* immigrants and migration
militaries: American primacy in, 57, 93, 102, 132–33; China and, 47–50, 52–54; Germany and, 84; India and, 52, 53, 77; international order and, 15–16, 44, 46, 50; Japan and, 81; modernization of, 40, 48, 55; openness strategy and, 96–99, 104–7, 111, 114–16, 132–33; regime transitions and, 24; Russia and, 48–49, 72, 108–9; tech sector and, 124; U.S. allies and, 51–52
misinformation. *See* disinformation; polarization
mixed regimes, 6, 59, 65, 87, 103, 106, 115, 148
Modi, Narendra, 74, 76
multipolarity, 4, 5, 14, 45, 53, 100, 106, 140; and alliances, 137; in Asia, 46–47, 52–54, 58–59, 77, 87; implications for diplomacy, 97, 131
Muslims targeted in India, 74

NAFTA (North American Free Trade Agreement), 112
Napoleon, 17
National Defense Strategy (NDS) Commission, 128
National Emerging Technology Council (NETC), 125–26
nationalism, 12, 20, 37
National Security Council, 134
National Security Strategy, 125, 128, 184n5
NATO. *See* North Atlantic Treaty Organization